ANGORA

a handbook
for spinners

Erica Lynne
drawings by Roberta Wackett

INTERWEAVE PRESS

Illustrations: Roberta Wackett
Production: Marc McCoy Owens

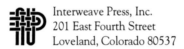 Interweave Press, Inc.
201 East Fourth Street
Loveland, Colorado 80537

Library of Congress Catalog Number 92-367
ISBN 0-934026-75-0

Library of Congress Cataloging-in-Publication Data:
    Lynne, Erica, 1953–
        Angora : a handbook for spinners / Erica Lynne.
            p.   cm.
        Includes bibliographical references and index.
        ISBN 0-934026-75-0 : $14.95
        1. Hand spinning.   2. Knitting—Patterns.   3. Angora rabbits.
    I. Title
    TT847.L96   1992
    746.1--dc20   92-367
                                                                     CIP

First printing: 4.5M:592:OVB

To the memory of
Uncle Van

Acknowledgments

When you write a book compiling the experiences of a decade, you become very much aware of all the people who have influenced you. Those whose contributions related directly to the subject are mentioned in the text. Although it is impossible to mention them all by name, I want to thank members of the Saturday Group of the Black Sheep Handspinners Guild for sharing all their knowledge and enthusiasm with me for so many years. Happy spinning to all of you.

To fiction writer Beth Wetherby, I am indebted for providing many valuable insights on writing. I want to thank Roberta Wackett for her patience, skill and exemplary artwork. The tedious job of proofreading was done uncomplainingly by Jacques Lewin. For their support in the countless ways that make a project of this magnitude possible, my heartfelt thanks go to Ellie, Steve, Christopher and Jacques.

The person who provided the inspiration for my art and my business, as well as for this book, was Francis J. Van Bortel, who shattered my life by his sudden death on New Year's Day 1989.

Table of Contents

Introduction

MORE THAN TEN YEARS AGO, I ATTENDED A THREE-DAY WORKSHOP ABOUT SILK. Among the items on display was a handspun, handknit vest, delicate, lacy, and soft. It was the most sumptuous fabric I'd ever felt, an exquisite blend of silk and angora.

That was my introduction to the luxury of angora. I'd heard of it, of course, but I didn't even know it came from rabbits. The biggest impression I took away from that workshop was that I had to find and raise angora rabbits.

In acquiring my first angoras, I made nearly every mistake possible. I bought the first rabbits I found, from a breeder I knew nothing about. The rabbits' fur was matted. They were all litter-mates, and their records showed a long history of sibling matings. I had no cages or food for them and no knowledge of how to comb, spin, or knit angora fiber. I just figured I'd find a book to learn from.

To my surprise and dismay, such books were not to be found. What was I going to do with my angoras? Rabbits, after all, don't sit on shelves like stored fibers. I did the best I could; I made mistakes and learned from them.

During the first years, the little information I located wasn't very helpful to me, a spinner with just a few rabbits. Some publications were too general or folksy. Others were geared toward large commercial rabbitries. Most emphasized rabbit raising, with only a paragraph or two about spinning. Expert texts on rabbits only lightly touched on angoras, and textile arts books merely mentioned angora as a specialty fiber.

This book is designed to introduce handspinners to the pleasures of angora. It presumes a basic knowledge of textile arts: spinning and knitting or weaving. It includes information on angora fiber characteristics, design, and care.

My primary goal is to provide the background knowledge and "how-to" instructions necessary to work successfully with angora. I've tried to include a wide range of ideas as inspiration for you to develop your own style. Finally, this book is built on a foundation of scientific research in the field of angora production, to help even experienced angora enthusiasts better understand these rabbits and their fiber.

It is the book I wish I'd had.

Angora:
the luxury fiber

AN OLD CHINESE PROVERB SAYS: "HE WHO HAS IMAGINATION WITHOUT LEARN-ing has wings, but no feet." Though flights of fancy are necessary, I have found that working without background knowledge of a subject hinders progress. Learning actually stimulates my imagination.

Rabbits are one of the most recently domesticated animals. In the grand scheme of world economics, they hold only a very tiny spot. Compared to other domestic animals, rabbit research has been limited and most of what has been done is not easily accessible to the American public. It is hidden in scientific journals and foreign language books. I have made a special effort to distill from these sources the information most important to fiber artists and present it in an understandable fashion. Other sections of this book rely more heavily on my own experience and opinions, but the emphasis in this section is documented and research-based information. Historical perspectives, fiber structure, and grades are subject whose importance looms larger the longer you work in the field. It forms the basis for our art.

ANGORA THROUGH THE AGES

Exploring the history of the angora rabbit is like going on a scavenger hunt, searching backward through time. In the process, new discoveries delight, historical figures come alive, and isolated fragments of knowledge begin to coalesce into a perspective on our whole earth's history. While learning the past of the angora rabbit, I have seen the dawn of evolution, experienced the Ice Age, and sailed the Mediterranean with the Phoenicians. I have visited ancient Rome and medieval Europe. I have learned that history is not a truth carved in stone, but a puzzle with many missing pieces—an interpretive guessing game. The tantalizing clues are bits of bone and snippets of writing. They are woven into the history of angora.

The most ancient relatives of modern rabbits hopped and hid in the bushes of Asia and North America 55 million years ago, during the Eocene Epoch. Dinosaurs were already extinct and the Age of Mammals had begun. It was not until 800,000 years ago, however, that the first fossil evidence of rabbits as we know them appeared.

Our modern day rabbit, like all domestic rabbits, is descended from the wild rabbit, *Oryctolagus cuniculus*, which made its first appearance during the Great Ice Age (which had intervals of more moderate temperatures). Although some hom-inids may have existed then, it would be another 790,000 years before *Homo sapiens* evolved to see this timid, furry creature with long ears. Until the end of the very last glaciation, the wild rabbit seems to have stayed in the Iberian peninsula, which is where Spain is today. That the rabbit did not spread quickly over the earth is not terribly surprising. Rabbits are homebodies who like to stay put. They actively dislike water, which borders three sides of the Iberian peninsula. The mountains to the north didn't constitute a friendly environment either, especially with those icy glaciers advancing every hundred thousand years or so. After nearly 800,000 years, rabbits had made it out of Iberia only as far as southern France, only to be hunted and eaten by the Cro Magnons, an early race of humans who appeared on the scene about 10,000 years ago. From this point on, the lives of rabbits became closely intertwined with the lives of people. Not only have people distributed rabbits to nearly all continents of the world, but they have bred into O. *cuniculus* more variations than into any other domestic animal besides the dog.

The first historical reference to rabbits occurs at about 1100 BC, when seafaring Phoenicians landed in Spain. There they found large numbers of a strange burrowing mammal, long-eared and furry. It reminded them of the hyrax of their own country and so called the new creature "*shepham*", the word for hyrax in their own language. Because rabbits were so common, the Phoenicians named the new land "*i-shepham-im*" (Land of Rabbits), which latinized becomes Hispania, then anglicized becomes Spain. Through this odd quirk of history, Spain was named.

The Phoenicians were fearless sailors who dared to travel where no other peoples would. Consequently they came to dominate trade in the Mediterranean, including Italy, Greece, Babylonia and North Africa. They were very likely responsible for the initial dispersal of rabbits to other areas of the world.

Rearing rabbits in captivity was the brainchild of Marcus Terentius Varro, a Roman antiquarian and man of letters who lived from 116 to 27 BC. He suggested keeping rabbits in the already-established leporaria. These were large gardens, surrounded by stone walls in which trapped hares were kept until needed for the stew pot. On the surface, these must have seemed like a good idea. The system worked well for hares, which after all *look* a lot like rabbits. Rabbits, however, are quite different from hares. For one thing, rabbits burrow underground warrens and nests (hares live only on the surface). Surely the rabbits also burrowed under the leporaria walls as well. It must have come as some surprise to those first experimenters in rabbit keeping to find their leporaria full of holes and empty of rabbits. Having escaped the stew pot, the rabbits would have had a grand time roaming free and populating the new countryside. Presumably, people learned to extend the stone walls of the leporaria underground to inhibit escapees.

However, keeping rabbits in leporaria does not constitute true domestication, because no specialized breeding programs took place and once in the leporaria, the rabbits still had to be hunted. This process would quickly kill off rabbits with any friendly or tame tendencies, while the wildest and shyest would escape to breed again. This sort of selection pressure is the exact opposite of what one wants in a domestic animal.

At first, it was surely the adult rabbits which were used for food, being larger and supplying more nutrition and sustenance. However, with the convenience of the wild rabbits kept in the leporaria and the decadence of Roman society, a new culinary delicacy was discovered. Essentially the "yuppie" food for ancient Rome, laurices were unborn or newly born rabbit babies, which were eaten whole. For this accounting of Roman taste, we can thank Pliny the Elder, who lived during the first century, AD. He also recorded the devastating eruption of Mount Vesuvius.

After isolated monasteries began to keep rabbits as a readily available source of meat, the monk's interest quickly turned to the laurices. Biological relationships were not well understood at that time (even beaver, because of their aquatic habits, were considered "fish"), and laurices could be eaten as "fish" on religious days of fasting. Some doubt must have arisen about the propriety of laurice consumption. In AD 590 at least one bishop expressed his disapproval of the practice of eating laurices during Lent.

French monks were probably responsible for the actual domestication of wild rabbits, which occurred sometime between the sixth and tenth centuries AD. In order for the monks to obtain a ready supply of laurices, it would have been necessary for them to keep the rabbits in cages and protect the breeding does. Under these conditions, tamer and friendlier rabbits would be selected for, being rather easier to care for and handle than wild ones. In 1249, there is recorded a transaction between two monasteries for the purchase of two pairs of breeding rabbits.

Rabbits soon become popular all over Europe. Drawings from 1393 show noble ladies hunting rabbits in a leporarium. In 1407 rabbits were being kept on islands. Their natural fear of water made islands an ideal place for their confinement. During the sixteenth century, even Queen Elizabeth had her own "rabbit islands".

The early development of new varieties of rabbits provides more evidence of deliberate breeding. The first recorded reference to a white rabbit came in 1530 in a painting by Titian called "Madonna with Rabbit". The middle of the sixteenth century also saw the development of other colors such as black and piebald, as well as a fourfold increase in size. During the next hundred years, silver-gray and blue rabbits appeared, and a fur industry came into being.

In 1708, Mortimer described a long-haired white rabbit in England he called "white shock Turkey rabbit"—shock apparently referring to the length of the hair. The hair of this rabbit quickly became popular as a textile fiber in Britain. Export of the rabbits was forbidden by law, so that the British could maintain a monopoly on the glorious new fiber. In spite of the prohibition, British sailors brought angora rabbits to Bordeaux, France, in 1723. France soon became the center of angora production and maintained that status for the next 250 years.

The origin of the angora rabbit is not certain. Most sources claim that it was developed in Turkey, like the angora goat. Certainly the British who brought the first angora rabbits to France claimed to have found them in Asia Minor. However, they may have made this claim in order to avoid prosecution. Although the word "angora" may refer to place of origin, it may also be just a generic term for long hair. Somewhat later, there is an account of a French monk who bred a long-haired race of rabbits from short-haired stock. He believed that it was the special environmental conditions under which he raised the rabbits which accounted for the increase in hair length. (Genetics was not a well-developed science at the time.) Once rabbits were domesticated and kept in a protected environment, the long-haired gene, surely a detriment to wild rabbits, could have been selected for and kept and bred into rabbits in many areas.

THE DEVELOPMENT OF ANGORA AS AN INDUSTRY

France

Angora raising in France was greatly encouraged by a philanthropic couple, M. and Mme. Lard, during the latter half of the nineteenth century. (Mme. Lard continued the work after her husband's death in 1869.) This couple raised angora rabbits and gave them away to peasant farmers. In return, the peasants gave back half of the baby bunnies they raised, so that these again could be given away. Mme. Lard also encouraged the cottage textile industry. She writes (translated from the French):

> My angora rabbits are pure white or gray-black. Every three months their silky fur is combed off, carded and spun on a great wheel. I give the yarn to school girls who, in their spare time or while tending flocks of sheep or goats, knit many angora items such as gloves, stocking, slippers, knee warmers, shirt fronts, etc. I visit the girls regularly and encourage their work with a wage proportional to the difficulty of the knitted item and their skill in knitting. These silky angora garments are excellent. The doctors recommend them for rheumatism and other ailments of this nature, as well as for people with weak and delicate natures. It is softer and warmer than woolen flannel. I sell these garments to tourists visiting the thermal springs at Aix.

The French called angora rabbits *lapins de soie* (silk rabbits) and *lapins de peigne* (combing rabbits). By 1865, French angora rabbits were described as having hair 10–12 cm long (about 4 inches). The hair was plucked or combed off. By the end of the 1800s France was producing ten metric *tons* annually of angora fiber. At this time there was only one spinning mill in France capable of handling the delicate fibers, so most of it was exported as raw fiber to Britain. The owner of the French mill, M. Patard-Chatelain, also kept angora rabbits and although the exact size of his herd or the number of employees is not stated, it must have been a fairly large operation because he does mention that each woman employee was in charge of 600 rabbits.

France continued to dominate the angora industry until well into the twentienth century, but problems were developing both internally and internationally. As recently as 1950, a single rabbit's fiber production was under 500 grams (just over one pound) per year. There was too much hand labor involved and a lack of expert knowledge about rabbit raising. Also the once-stable international angora market had become quite volatile.

To rescue their angora industry, the French government established four national organizations with the following goals: to improve fiber quality and production, to promote general research on angoras, to study angora diseases in particular, and to maintain official pedigrees. Some of the most significant contributions to understanding angora and fiber production have been made in France.

The French industry is currently stabilized at about 100 metric tons per year, most of which is produced by small country farmers with 50 to 250 rabbits in each herd. Mme. Yvonne Joffre, a typical angora raiser, lives on a farm in the French countryside. She and her husband raise much of their own food, collect wild herbal medications in the fields, and rely on a herd of 3000 meat rabbits for income. Until a bad back forced her to sell them, Mme. Joffre also raised 70 angora rabbits. The rabbits were kept in modern cages. Only the minimum number of bucks necessary for reproduction were kept, and only a few of the does are bred each year, as highest quality fiber and best production come from unbred does. Mme. Joffre plucked her angoras on a special table, using a plucking knife. Like many other angora producers in France, she sold her angora fiber to a marketing cooperative which pays a low set price for the fiber with extra dividends based on current world market prices. Fiber production has been raised to about one kilogram (2.2 pounds) of fiber per rabbit per year. Interestingly enough, the price of an adult angora rabbit is based on the market price of angora—the price of the rabbit is set at the current market price of one kilogram of fiber.

Angora production is not limited to France. In fact, there is a substantial world trade in angora fiber. Czechoslovakia rivals France both in the level of production and quality of fiber, producing 80 to 120 metric tons per year. Smaller amounts of good quality fiber are produced in the England, Spain, Switzerland, Poland, and Belgium.

Latter 19th century angora rabbits. An illustration from Lièvres, Lapins, et Léporides, *by Eugene Gayot. 1865.*

The Orient

China currently dominates the world market, producing around 2000 metric tons (5 million pounds!) of angora annually. Chinese angora tends to be of different quality than French or Czech angora. Softer, finer and shorter, it is most often blended with higher grade angora (for 100% angora garments) or with other fibers, (such as wool, silk or synthetics) because it is not substantial enough to be used alone. Angora-blend garments from Chinese fiber are inexpensive and readily available. Unfortunately, the short angora sheds, and the blends are a sad substitute for high fashion angora. Thus, angora tends to have a bad reputation with the general public. As the industry develops, better nutrition and more selective breeding may improve the quality of Chinese angora.

Japan and the Republic of Korea (as well as Argentina and India) also produce this "blending grade" angora. The large amount of angora produced in countries where hand labor is still relatively cheap has contributed to the instability of international angora trade.

Several years ago, I had a visit from Mr. Lee Hyung Won, who provided a glimpse into Korean angora raising. Mr. Lee runs a menswear store in Seoul but dreams of moving to the country and raising angora rabbits. He was greatly interested in my German angoras, the barn full of a hundred rabbits, and the rustic farm where a woman ran the business and the men cooked.

It was a fascinating visit for me as well. Mr. Lee described Korean rabbitries housing as many as 3000 angoras in hugh slate or vinyl barns five stories high. Their cages are less than half the size of ours. All of the angora rabbits in Korea are shorn. When he showed his friends in Korea my article in *Rabbits* magazine describing how to pluck angoras, they were horrified. Korea, he told us proudly, produced around ten tons of angora each year and imported even more for its flourishing garment industry. Mr. Lee also told us that Koreans eat most of the world's production of hot peppers. When it was all over we exchanged gifts—angora sweaters, of course!

Germany

One country which utilizes essentially all the angora it produces in its own domestic industry is West Germany. German angora is shorn, rather than plucked. The majority of the 30 to 40 tons produced each year is used in a 50/50 blend with Merino wool for long underwear. Sometimes rayon is added to the blend. Angora has long been known to remedy the pain of arthritis and rheumatism by keeping muscles and joints warm and dry. In Germany, the angora rabbit is also know as *menschenheilkaninchen* (the mystical magical human healing rabbit) for this reason. The long underwear is very popular in Europe. A limited amount of pure angora is used for fine sweaters, handknitting yarn, and medical underwear.

The Germans use low-grade angora for felted angora/wool blankets. Marketed as "health-blankets", they are made of a layer of angora and a layer of wool, bordered with silk. One German angora breeder invented a mattress pad filled with pure angora. Both are especially valued because they are warm and have the ability to breathe, and because angora can absorb twice the moisture of wool and still feel warm.

West Germany is also recognized for the astounding success of its angora rabbit breeding programs. Angora rabbits from France were introduced to Germany in 1777. After the First World War, country people took to raising a few angora rabbits to supplement their scanty incomes. During the '20s and '30s, some of the best German zoologists became interested in angora production. Much research was done, and the first testing stations were established after World War II. At these testing stations, angora rabbits were evaluated for the quality and quantity of fiber produced over time (about three months). Also established was a Registry of Excellent Angora Raisers—the German version of the National Angora Rabbit

Breeders Club, except with more explicit goals and strict membership requirements. These efforts yielded enormous improvements in fiber production, with some of the record holders now producing nearly four pounds of angora per year—four times the productions of the early 1900s.

With a strong modern economy, angora raising in Germany now is primarily competitive in spirit, with breeders vying for top honors with the highest producing rabbits, and trying to break fiber production records. This competition is well supported by a healthy angora textile industry.

The United States

The first records of angora being produced in the United States date back to the early 1930s. During this decade, a commercial angora herd was established in California, and the first specialty club was formed. Refugees from World War I may have brought their skills in the angora trade to this country. By 1938 there were several angora cooperatives and plans for a spinning mill in Colorado. Unfortunately for the infant American angora industry, the price of angora fiber suddenly dropped dramatically. The spinning mill was never built and most of the large commercial breeders went out of business. Since then, angoras have been raised primarily as fancy show animals in the United States.

An angora textile industry may be impossible in the United States for the same reason that the silk industry failed to thrive here—both require too much expensive hand labor. Instead, the increasing interest in natural fibers and the desire of more Americans to own and operate their own small businesses has resulted in a small but thriving trade in luxury angora wear in which the quality, elegance, and custom design work of handspun and handmade garments take precedence over mass production.

ANGORA RABBITS AND THEIR FIBER

In reference to textiles, the term "angora" *always* refers to the fiber from angora rabbits. Because the word has also been applied to long-haired goats (which produce mohair fiber), the International Organization for Standardization has changed "angora" goat to mohair goat. Many people call angora "wool", but I prefer not to use the term because angora fiber is technically hair, rather than wool. Though it resembles sheep's wool in some ways, angora is unique among textile fibers. With an understanding of special structure and textile characteristics you will be prepared to make knowledgeable decisions when designing with angora.

Fiber Characteristics

Remember your first magnifying lens? How fascinating it was to examine your fingernail, a snowflake, a dead mosquito! That simple plastic toy entertained me for hours. As an older child, I viewed algae, protozoans, and the cellular structure of plants and animals through the complex lenses of the school microscopes. By the time I finished college, I was using electron microscopes large enough to fill a small room. These state-of-the-art instruments use an electron beam, rather than light, to illuminate the subject, and magnetic fields instead of glass lenses to focus the beam. Among the microorganisms I was supposed to be studying, I slipped in some fiber samples. The most dramatic pictures came from the scanning electron microscope, which illuminated the surface structure in vivid 3-D. Hours slipped by unnoticed as I viewed angora, cashmere, silk and more.

A microscope, or even a hand lens, can show you a lot about fiber structure. Take a moment now and look at some plucked angora fiber, if you have some available. You should be able to find three kinds of hairs, each with a different form. Three different types of hair! Here already is a big difference between angora and sheep wool, which generally has only one fiber type.

Wool is homogeneous, meaning that all its fibers are of the same type. Because it has several different fiber types, angora is described as heterogeneous. The heterogeneity of angora fleece is responsible for some of its special properties. Let's take a closer look.

Return to your angora sample. Pick out a fiber which is one of the longest, thickest, and stiffest. If you were describing it, you would probably call this fiber a hair. If you do not have any fleece to look at right now you can study the drawings at right. These strong stiff hairs are called bristles or erector hairs. On very close inspection, one can see that these hairs are flame shaped. The root is embedded in the skin, and bears a slender body, an enlarged head, and a pointed tip.

Bristles are the longest, widest and least numerous of the three types. They can reach 4 inches or more in length at maturity and are up to 100 microns in diameter at the widest part of the head. Bristles are attached to tiny muscles which, when contracted, cause them to become erect. Bristles are dispersed throughout the fleece and allow the rabbit to control the loft of his fur; when the hairs are erect the fleece fluffs up, increasing dead air space and thus insulating capacity. Some researchers separate bristles into two smaller groups: regular bristles and tylotriches, which are slightly larger and are thought to have a sensory function.

An abundance of thin, wispy fibers form the downy undercoat which insulates the rabbit. The best down has a gentle wavy crimp. Its fineness (Merino wool is 30% thicker) is what makes angora so soft and wonderful to touch. By far the most abundant fiber type on a rabbit, down fibers at maturity are 2½ to 3 inches long

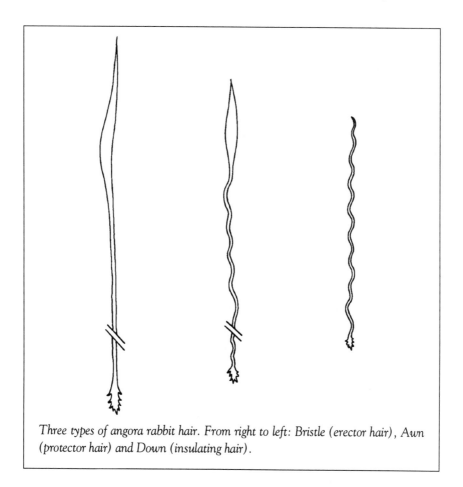

Three types of angora rabbit hair. From right to left: Bristle (erector hair), Awn (protector hair) and Down (insulating hair).

and have an even, circular diameter of 10 to 15 microns. The heads are not swollen.

Now look for hairs which seem halfway between bristles and down. These *awns*, or *protector hairs* have hairy, wide heads 50 to 80 microns wide) and thin, crimpy bodies (10 to 30 microns). The large heads, poorly supported by the thin bodies, tend to fall over, forming a protective covering for the fleece.

Both the bristles and the awns have rigid, slippery heads, and are commonly referred to collectively as "guard hair" by rabbit raisers. On the rabbit, these hairs cover the down. Foreign particles slip easily off this protective coat. Guard hairs are not as soft as down and some people consider them undesirable. But just as they perform important functions for the rabbits, so do they enhance a textile project by adding strength and helping prevent felting. The ends of these hairs readily slip out of the yarn and form a substantial foundation for the halo of down fluff which characterizes quality handspun angora.

Internally, each fiber is composed of three layers: the cuticle, the cortex; and the medulla. The cuticle is the outermost layer which protects the hair. It is formed by two layers of overlapping scales, like tiles on a roof, with the free edges pointing toward the tip. You may already be familiar with the scale pattern on sheep wool. For the rabbits, these overlapping scales help prevent foreign particles from entering the fleece and they facilitate the removal of any which do penetrate. In yarn production, scales increase the friction necessary to hold fibers together. Because rabbit hair has an unusually smooth cuticle, it makes a slippery yarn. In part, angora owes its softness and downy halo to the cuticle, which feels comfortable next to the skin and allows the fiber ends to slip easily from the yarn, forming the characteristic aureole.

Situated under the cuticle, the cortex is composed of microscopic, spindle-shaped *fibrils* which are packed together tightly and embedded in an semi-solid glue-like protein. This two-part structure gives strength, elasticity, and flexibility to the hair.

One way to visualize the internal structure of the cortex is to compare it to your handspun yarn. As fibers are spun into singles, and singles are plied into yarn, *microfibrils* are "glued" together to form *macrofibrils*, which are glued together to form the cortex.

In rabbits (and in sheep and other mammals) both the cuticle and the cortex are composed primarily of keratin—an organic compound relatively resistant to acids, but easily damaged by alkalis and oxidants. This is why you can use limited amounts of vinegar or acetic acid when dyeing without damage to the fiber, while alkalis (some soaps and detergents and the chemicals used in indigo and orchil lichen dyeing) and oxidants (bleaches) pose more problems. The keratin molecule has many reactive sites (places which easily bind to other molecules such as dyes). Keratin can also absorb up to 33% of its own weight in water without feeling wet, which allows the wearer to stay warm, dry and comfortable.

The central hollow core of the fiber is called the medulla. In angora, it is composed primarily of air-tight cubical chambers stacked one atop another in a single row. Under the microscope, this medullar structure appears ladder-like. At the tips of the guard hairs, the medulla becomes inflated, filling the enlarged heads with irregular chambers like bubbles.

Most down fibers, including sheep's wool, don't have a hollow core. The medulla gives angora some special characteristics, affecting its warmth, weight, dyeability, and appearance.

These air pockets increase the insulating capacity of the fiber without adding extra weight. Some studies have shown angora to be as much as eight times warmer than an equivalent weight of wool. The angora fiber is actually less dense than wool, meaning that it has less mass per unit volume. (This is what people mean

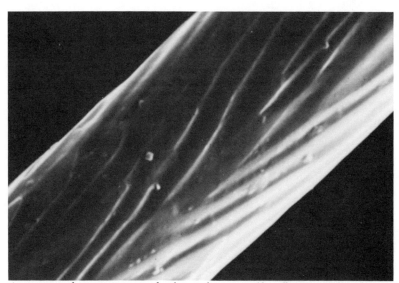

A scanning electron micrograph of a single angora fiber illustrating the relatively smooth, chevron shaped cuticle scales. Magnification: 1200X.

Photo by Erica Lynne. SEM facilities courtesy of State University of New York College of Environmental Science and Forestry, Syracuse, NY.

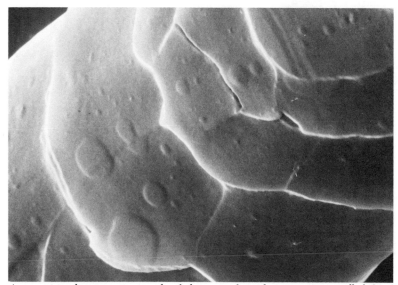

A scanning electron micrograph of sheep wool, with contrasting, well defined cuticle scales. Magnification: 400X.

Photo by Erica Lynne. SEM facilities courtesy of State University of New York College of Environmental Science and Forestry, Syracuse, NY.

when they say that angora is "light weight"). A filmy angora sweater is surprisingly warm.

The medulla also affects the way that angora takes dye. You may have heard that angora is difficult to dye. This is not due to any chemical properties, but because angora is difficult to wet thoroughly and because the medulla is hollow. (Air pockets can't bind any dye.) The enlarged heads of the "guard hairs" tend to take less dye than the rest of the fiber and as they are the ends which slip out of the yarn, their lighter color actually enhances the nimbus effect.

A longitudinal cross-section of an angora down fiber showing the "ladder" type medulla—a central core filled with hollow cubicles—which greatly increases insulating capacity.

Angora fiber is 99% pure, right as it comes off the rabbit. Compare that to wool, in which half or more of the weight of the fleece may be impurities. There are three main reasons why angora is so pure and clean. First, the sebaceous glands (which produce the "grease" in sheep wool) are hypoactive. In other words, mostly they don't do much. The sebaceous glands in rabbits produce only the minimum amount of "grease" necessary to lubricate the growing hair and that is really a very small amount. Rabbits have few sweat glands and none under the long, spinnable hairs. In fact, they have no sweat glands on the main parts of their bodies. Finally, frequent grooming by the rabbit itself keeps the angora fleece clean. Angora is so pure and clean that the commercial angora industry uses angora fiber just as it comes off the rabbit, with none of the initial scouring or chemical treatments used on wool. The industry depends on this high rate of purity and premium prices are paid for clean angora. It should be noted that residual rabbit saliva on unwashed fibers may cause allergic reactions in some individuals. Commercial angora products are, of course, washed before being marketed to consumers.

Angora hair, for all its other properties, would be of little value to the textile industry were it not for its length. Unlike hair color, which is controlled by many pairs of genes, hair length is controlled by only a single pair, designated by the twelfth letter of the alphabet: "L" (short hair) and "l" (long hair). "L" is capitalized because short hair is *dominant* over long hair, which is *recessive*. There are three possible combinations "LL", "Ll", or "ll". Rabbits with "LL" and "Ll" have short hair. In order to have long (angora) hair, a rabbit must have "ll".

Rather than increasing the rate of growth, the "l" gene increases the amount of time the fiber spends growing before it is naturally shed. It is probably present in small numbers (hidden by the dominant "L") in wild rabbit populations. Presumably it is selected against in nature because the long hair would hinder the movements of the rabbit who needs to move quickly to escape predators and also would become matted, wet, and dirty, promoting disease. With the protection from predators and environmental extremes offered by domestication, this long-haired rabbit can flourish and provide us with magnificent fiber.

BIOLOGICAL FACTS ABOUT ANGORAS

Surely rabbits are one of America's favorite animals, with the Easter Bunny, Peter Rabbit, Br'er Rabbit and others filling the stories and songs of our childhood culture. There are even Harvey, Bugs, and more recently, Roger Rabbit, to entertain us. But fairy tales and story books tell us little of what to expect from a real live rabbit.

Most people know that rabbits are timid, furry creatures, with long ears and a sensitive nose, which hop around. After I'd had angora rabbits for a while, questions kept popping into my head. Why is rabbit hair so clean, when sheep wool is dirty and greasy? Why does the hair come out in patches, rather than all at once? What kinds of things encourage fiber growth? Will feeding them more give me more fiber or fat rabbits? For those of you who, like me, want to know where rabbits fit in the grand scheme of things and the reasons behind the facts, this section is written. It covers some of the basic biology of the rabbit which you might find interesting if you have one for a pet, as well as some background information about the way it produces that wonderful stuff—angora.

Taxonomy

Rabbits are gnawers. They used to be classed with another group of gnawers, the order Rodentia—an enormous group which includes beavers, squirrels, prairie dogs, woodchucks, mice, and rats. Taxonomic biologists have since moved rabbits and hares into their own order: Lagomorpha, and family: Leporidae, based on some especially interesting features. These characteristics include differences in the skull and tooth configuration, the inability of rabbits to use their front feet as "hands", and the rabbits' unique digestive system. Hares and rabbits are often confused. This confusion is complicated by many common names of rabbits and hares: The jack rabbit is really a hare and the Belgian hare is really a rabbit.

Hares are usually larger than rabbits, with larger ears and feet. They escape from their predators by bounding away quickly rather than by hiding. Hare babies are born fully furred and with their eyes open. They are ready to move about and follow their mother within a few minutes of birth.

Rabbits, on the other hand, build fur-lined nests for their babies, which are born blind, naked, and helpless. The European rabbit, *Oryctolagus cuniculus*, formed the foundation stock for all domestic rabbits. European rabbits are communal animals, living in large systems of underground tunnels called warrens. (*Cuniculus*, in Latin, means underground tunnel.) The droppings are usually deposited at a communal site, presumably to keep their underground homes clean. This tendency for wild rabbits to place their droppings in a specific place allows us to litter-train domestic rabbits.

In the United States, wild rabbits belong to an entirely different genus, *Sylvilagus*. American cottontail rabbits do not burrow, but build their nests on the ground. I remember my delight and surprise at finding a nest of tiny babies right on the lawn of my childhood home. The really amazing thing was that the nest was completely invisible from a distance of only a few feet. I had found it only because I was mowing the lawn. Of course, I mowed around it.

Physical Traits of Angora Rabbits

As any gardener knows, rabbits are vegetarians. In the wild, rabbits nibble on buds, grass, and leaves, and gnaw on the bark or twigs of trees. In our gardens, they can destroy whole rows of lettuce or greens. Wild rabbits live entirely on fresh plant material and often do not even need to drink because there is so much water in the food they consume. Domestic rabbits which are fed primarily dry pellets must be given plenty of water and can only be fed greens cautiously, because their complex digestive systems are not adjusted to fresh food.

Rabbits have an unusual digestive system—one of the main reasons they earned a separate category from the rodents. Some of rabbit digestion is accomplished by intestinal bacteria, much like cows, sheep, or other ruminants. Through an odd evolutionary quirk, the digestive bacteria in rabbits are located in the appendix and caecum, which are lower in the digestive tract than the area where digested nutrients can be absorbed into the body. Rabbits deal with this unusual state of affairs by passing some of the food they eat through the digestive tract two or more times. This practice is called coprophagy, which is to say that rabbits eat some of their own droppings. However, they do this in an efficient, systematic manner, by producing two different types of droppings.

Droppings produced in the very early morning (called "night droppings") are soft and coated with a layer of mucus. They contain particles of undigested food and intestinal bacteria. "Droppings" is not an accurate term for these excretions, because they are not dropped. The rabbit twists around and eats them directly as they are excreted. Some of the nutrients may be recycled two, three, or four times. In addition, the bacteria in the "night droppings" contribute protein and vitamins. During other times of the day, the more commonly-seen "hard" pellets are produced. These represent the true waste product of rabbit digestion and are not reingested.

Everyone knows that rabbits are quiet creatures, but few people besides rabbit raisers realize that rabbits have a considerable vocabulary for an animal which is thought not to make a sound. A doe guarding her nest can growl as menacingly as any dog. A rabbit that is hurt or frightened can emit ear-piercing squeals. Sometimes a baby rabbit will squeal as if his life were coming to an end, even if you pick him up very gently. A recently mated doe whimpers like a puppy and a mating buck snorts loudly after copulation. In addition to vocalizations, rabbits make noise by thumping their hind legs. These loud thumps are warning signals, like a beaver slapping its tail on the water.

Rabbits mature at about six months of age. The height of the breeding season of wild rabbits runs from January to June. Many domestic rabbits can be bred year round, but it is easier to breed them during their evolutionarily, correct season. A doe may breed from four to eight times a year with three to eight bunnies per litter. Productivity in many domestic breeds of rabbits is even higher. It doesn't take a lot of arithmetic skill to see how quickly these animals could overpopulate an area where there were no predators to keep their numbers in check. Were they able to evade their various predators, rabbits could live up to seven or eight years. Few live longer than a year or two in the wild.

Hair Growth

As handspinners and textile artists, we are interested primarily in the hairs that animals produce. We tend to have an odd perspective on these fibers. We view them as something grown especially for us. We forget that mammals existed millions of years before we humans came on the scene and that they grow their coats not for our convenience, but for their own comfort and protection. Understanding how and why the fibers grow to suit the needs of their original owners broadens our perspective by increasing our understanding of fiber characteristics and animal husbandry practices. It provides a solid basis of knowledge from which we can analyze new information and separate fact from fiction.

The textile fibers we covet provide the rabbit or other mammal with insulation, comfort, and protection. These hairs are subject to wear and damage due to exposure to sun, wind, rain, and abrasion. Once it is extruded from the skin, hair is not composed of living material and cannot heal itself. Hair must be replaced at regular intervals if it is to continue to function in a beneficial way. In addition, hair replacement must occur in a manner which does not leave a wild animal entirely denuded at any one time.

Hair growth and replacement is accomplished within a structure called a hair follicle, which is a tiny pocket in the epidermis. It originates deep in the dermal layer of the skin. Look at this figure of a typical hair follicle. The basic parts of the hair follicle include the hair bulb, the dermal papilla, and the internal and external sheaths. The basal hair bulb is the structure which produces the new cells for the growing hair. The dermal papilla contains blood vessels which provide nourishment for the bulb. The internal and external sheaths participate in the development, formation, and shape of the hair in complex ways, not all of which are entirely understood.

There are several accessory structures as well. The arrector pili muscle is a very tiny muscle which connects the hair follicle with the surface of the epidermis. It

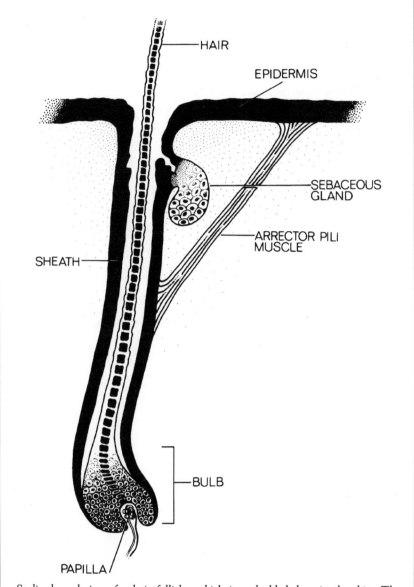

HAIR

EPIDERMIS

SEBACEOUS GLAND

ARRECTOR PILI MUSCLE

SHEATH

BULB

PAPILLA

Stylized rendering of a hair follicle, which is embedded deep in the skin. The epidermis is the top layer of skin. Connective tissue and fat deposits surround the follicle. At the base, the bulb, with its proliferating cells, is supplied by nourishing blood vessels.

raises the mature hair in response to cold or fright. Erect hairs provide more trapped air for insulation from the cold and also make the wearer appear larger and more frightening. Visualize the chickadee with its feathers fluffed up against the winter cold or a hissing cat with its hair standing on end. Although we humans no longer have fur over all our skin, we still experience the contraction of arrector pili muscles as "goose bumps". Changes in contraction of the arrector pili muscle during hair growth may also be responsible for fiber crimp.

There are two glands which usually accompany a hair follicle. The sebaceous gland makes lubricants which facilitate the movement of the hair as it grows up through the follicle and also provide a protective coating for the hair fiber. In sheep, it is responsible for the lanolin and "grease" in wool. Sweat glands produce moisture for temperature regulation. Both of these glands are largely inactive in rabbits. Rabbit sebaceous glands produce just barely enough lubricant to slide the growing hair out of the follicle. Rabbits cool themselves through capillary dilation in their ears, panting, and positioning rather than by the evaporation of sweat.

The basal follicular bulb interests us most as textile artists, because it is the direct source of all our mammalian fibers. Cells within the hair bulb have an unlimited capacity for producing new cells by a process called mitosis, or cell division. During embryonic development, all cells in the body have the capacity to divide and produce new cells. In a mature body, this capacity is much more limited, either to specific areas, such as hair or nails, or to specific times, such as when needed for wound healing. Some cells, the spinal nerves in humans for instance, cannot divide even in order to heal themselves. When cell multiplication rages out of control we call it cancer. So it is a special group of cells in the hair bulb which produces the fibers we covet. It is because these cells can multiply indefinitely that we can pluck the hairs out, even by the roots, and still be assured of a new harvest of angora fiber.

In spite of the hair bulb's ongoing capacity for cell division, it usually does not grow hair continuously. Instead, follicles alternate between stages of active hair growth and inactive states when the hairs are mature and later fall out. This system limits the length of the hair and allows for the replacement of worn and damaged hair. Most domestic sheep are the major exception to this rule. They have continuously active follicles and must depend on humans to relieve them annually of their excess wool. Because they are the textile-producing animal most familiar to handspinners, this can lead to misunderstandings about the cycles of hair growth in other mammals. So clear your mind of your sheep-raising experiences and try to imagine the situation of another mammal, a little wild rabbit, for example.

There has been a lot of research on hair growth, some of which has been done on rabbits. Other studies have been done on rats, mice, and cows, among others. The results for these fur-bearing mammals is usually considered applicable to other fur-bearing animals as well. It is the compilation of all these studies which give us an increasingly more detailed understanding of hair growth.

The active stage of follicle growth is often referred to by scientists studying hair growth as anagen, and the mature resting stage as telogen. There are several stages in between; their number and names depend on which researcher is describing them. In general, hair growth begins with an embryonic stage. All the activity of the embryonic stage takes place below the level of the skin. It consists of reorganization of the follicle bulb in preparation for hair production and the early differentiation of the inner hair sheath and the tip of the hair. Next follows a period of rapid growth of the hair shaft. The rate of growth in this period is five to ten times the rate during the embryonic stage. As the hair shaft grows, the cells differentiate, so that they develop the structures and chemical composition particular to that type of hair. When growth and differentiation are complete, there is a mature hair fully anchored in its resting follicle bed.

The duration of the active phase of hair growth determines the length of the hair follicle in rabbits. Short-haired rabbits have an active stage of about five weeks. Anagen (the active stage) continues for about 13 weeks in angora rabbits. The duration of anagen is genetically predetermined. It is constant for each individual follicle, although there is variation between follicles.

In contrast, the length of time a follicle remains inactive can he highly variable. Initiation of a new growth phase may take place within a few days, or the follicle may remain dormant for months. In this manner, wild animals can regulate density of hair as needed for different seasons. The factors which determine the onset of a new active phase include: the internal (genetic) follicular cycle, environmental conditions such as day length, physiological factors such as hormones and nutrition, and mechanical factors such as plucking.

A wild animal living in a temperate climate needs a heavier coat in winter than in summer. Except for *extreme* cold, temperatures do not usually affect fur production. Instead, seasonal changes are due primarily to the changing length, of the day. It is the relative amount of daylight which influences the physiology of the animal. In angora rabbits, the increasing day length of spring causes a decrease in fiber production of about 30%. After the late winter shedding period, some of the follicles enter a fallow period which can last for months. During this time, these follicles don't produce any hair at all. Follicles which are active in summer produce shorter, finer hairs. Decreasing day length in late summer and fall reactivates dormant follicles, and stimulates an increase in fiber length and diameter.

Biochemistry

Good nutrition is essential for luxuriant growth of hair. Research shows that animals with poor nutrition delay their shedding and hair replacement. Hair growth requires energy and nutrients supplied from food, so delaying hair replacement becomes a conservative measure for animals that are not well fed. Consequently, inadequate nutrition results in lower fiber production.

The positive effects of quality nutrition are limited by the animal's genetic capacity. Each angora rabbit is born with a maximum fiber production level built into its genes. Over-feeding of calories (carbohydrates or proteins) cannot increase fiber production above this level.

Hormones are chemical messengers which are carried in the blood and control many of the physiological systems which keep all animals functioning, ourselves included. Commonly-known hormones include insulin, which regulates blood sugar level and estrogens, which influence reproductive cycles. Hormones may stimulate an action or inhibit it, and there are hormones which do both for the initiation of hair growth in follicles.

Thyroid hormones stimulate anagen in hair follicles. Leslie Samson of Canada communicated to me several years ago the interesting fact that blood tests on her German angora rabbits showed much higher levels of thyroid hormones than were expected. Perhaps this is connected in some way to the higher production of this breed.

Adrenocorticotropic hormones tend to inhibit the initiation of anagen. These are the hormones which are released in response to fright, stress, danger, and some diseases. In sheep, these hormones cause the breaks or "tenderness" in wool fibers resulting from illness or stress. This provides a rationale for the common advice to keep rabbits healthy and stress-free for the best fiber production, since stress automatically releases these hormones which interfere with fiber production.

Another group of hormones which inhibit the onset of anagen are the androgens and estrogens, the sex hormones from both the male and the female. This could be an additional cause of decreased fiber production in pregnant does. It is sometimes recommended that castrated males be kept as "woolers". Castration of males (which abruptly interferes with androgen production) initiates hair growth. Subsequently, however, normal patterns of hair growth resume.

Removal of the hair shaft by plucking stimulates the production of new hair. One study (on rats, but probably generally applicable to rabbits) showed that plucking the hair as soon as it was mature advanced new follicular activity by nine days. The degree of advancement lessened the longer the mature hair was allowed to remain in place. Once the hair is plucked, there is a lapsed time of three days before cell division takes place, and the new tips appear after another five days. So it takes more than a week for new hair to appear on the skin of an animal after it is plucked. This should reassure breeders, to whom it appears that their rabbit will be naked "forever".

That plucking should stimulate the initiation of anagen makes sense in terms of a wild animal's survival: It needs to replace lost hair as soon as possible. When a hair is plucked out by the root, a bit of the living material may come out with it. However, because the cells of the hair bulb are infinitely capable of cell division, plucking does not keep new hairs from growing. In fact, the exact opposite occurs.

In young developing mammals, the growth and production of hair in the hair follicles is synchronous, which is to say that all the follicles are producing hair at the same stage in the cycle at the same time. As mammals mature, this synchrony is gradually lost, presumably because it is a disadvantage for the animal to lose all its hair at once. In some animals, like humans and guinea pigs, the shedding and replacement of hair is continuous and random. Each follicle replaces hair independently of any other follicle. In other animals, such as rodents and rabbits, hair replacement occurs in a pattern of shedding and regrowth in small patches of fur. Angora rabbit raisers have often noted that an animal may need to be plucked over a period of several days and that some areas of fur seem to come out while other stick tightly—a phenomenon which clearly illustrates the asynchronous follicular activity. Regular plucking at the proper time not only shortens the time lapse between the growth of the new hairs, but also restores the follicular synchrony so that a greater proportion of the fur will be ready to pluck at the same time. This is a great convenience to angora rabbit raisers. Shearing does not influence follicular activity and therefore neither shortens the lag time between growth cycles nor promotes follicular synchrony. In addition, because the follicles are producing hairs at different stages of growth at different times, hairs lacking their integral structure will be harvested when shorn. The differences between plucked and shorn angora fiber as they affect handspun yarn and fabrics are discussed below.

TYPES AND GRADES OF ANGORA

If you have seen angora only from, say, a simple sales booth or one rabbit raiser, you may not be aware of the many kinds, colors, and qualities of angora fiber available. In the early years, I struggled through many disappointing "learning experiences". It took years of spinning to become aware of all the distinctions. The breed and age of the rabbit, fiber length, and even the method of harvesting influence the textile properties of angora. Whether you raise your own angora or buy it, the following information should help you avoid costly errors.

All angora is not equal. It should be separated into grades based on its suitability for specific projects. The system I developed (first published in *Rabbits* magazine in 1983) is particularly suited to handspinners' needs. With minor variations (mostly finer subdivisions), I still use the same system today. Design uses of these grades are discussed in the chapters on yarn and garment design.

Grading angora implies that value judgments are being made. In spite of this, we know that any given characteristic has value *only in relation to its end use*. Keep in mind your own ideas as you evaluate and select angora for your project. Remember that "prime" or "first quality" may not always be what you want in order to create a desired effect.

Grade 1: Prime Fiber

Grade 1 angora consists of prime plucked fibers, at least 2½ (preferably 3) inches long and absolutely free of matts or tangles. Angora is a slippery fiber and without that length, will shed in the finished fabric. Only perfectly clean, adult fibers are permissible. There are no cut fibers, and no tangles from combing. Ideally, these fibers all lie parallel in locks just as they were plucked off the rabbit. There is absolutely no wasted fiber. Without carding or any other method of fiber preparation, grade 1 angora can be readily drafted and spun with good control. The use of grade 1 angora maximizes the characteristic furry halo of the best high fashion angora, while minimizing shedding and felting.

Grade 2: Combings

Grade 2 angora includes unmatted combed fibers, plucked fibers less than 2½ inches in length, and shorn fibers more than 2 inches long. It must be absolutely clean and from adult rabbits. The combed fibers are obtained during routine grooming and the combing that is done just prior to plucking. In addition to the end tangles put into the fibers by the comb itself, there may be small amounts of tangled fibers from the rabbit. The combed fibers are intact, but the tangles interfere with easy, controlled drafting. There must be no matted or felted fibers. On many angora rabbits, the hair on the dewlap (under the chin and on the chest) and from the belly will be shorter than 2½ inches at maturity. Plucked angora from these areas goes into grade 2, as well as long clipped fiber.

Given my preference for plucked fiber, you might wonder why I would ever have long-staple clipped angora. The most common reason is that I must sometimes shear the animals down completely in the heat of summer. An extended heat

Prime, plucked angora fiber is at least 2½ inches long, clean and absolutely free of matts or tangles. Fibers should be kept as parallel as possible.

wave causes the animals undue suffering and clipping off the fleece is one way to provide relief. All of these types of fibers are almost, but not quite, good enough for grade 1. With carding, these fibers can be used in blends with fine wools and silks.

Grade 3: Other Spinnable Fibers

Grade 3 consists of everything else that is spinnable: matted combings, short shorn fibers, stained fibers, fibers contaminated with small amounts of vegetable matter, and those from bunnies under a year old, whether plucked or shorn. These fibers are used to create tweedy blends with medium grade wools. The wool keeps the shorter angora fibers from shedding out and prevents baby fibers from matting. The little matts of angora add attractive slubs to the yarn, the stains wash away, and most of the straw of chaff will fall out during carding. Grade 3 angora adds softness and warmth to wool, but fluffs up only a little.

Heavily matted and felted angora is useless.

After developing my own grading system, I was interested to learn that the commercial standards for high-quality angora are similar to mine. Top grade angora in Germany is described as 6 cm long (about 2½ inches!), clean and unmatted. The French standards insist on a minimum length of 6 cm, clean, unmatted fibers, with guard hairs. (Remember, the French are striving for the furry look.) In 1948, the U.S. standards called for top grade angora to be from 5.4 to 7.2 cm in length, clean and unmatted. Lower grades in all three systems were based primarily on decreasing length. All commercial top grade angora is white and most (except the French) is shorn.

Harvesting Methods

The method of fiber harvesting has tangible, explainable, and dramatic effects on the textile properties of angora. There are three basic ways of parting a rabbit from its hair. Plucking involves pulling the hair out by its roots during natural shedding times. Combing also removes the fiber by the roots, but uses a tool which crimps and tangles the hairs, making them more difficult to draft and spin. Shorn, clipped, or cut angora is harvested with manual scissors or electric clippers. It is structurally different from plucked fiber.

When angora hair is plucked at maturity, it has achieved the length, dimensions and specific characteristics of the heterogenous fleece described earlier. Its guard hairs produce the loftiest yarn with a minimum of shedding. The slippery heads support yarn loft, while the thinner bodies hold the fiber in the yarn. Plucking also yields the longest fibers, which contributes to yarn stability.

All the hairs on baby bunnies begin and cease growing at approximately the same time. The mechanical action of the plucking stimulates simultaneous new hair growth and the production of a mature fleece every 13 weeks. Subsequent fleeces will have the same structure and quality as the first.

When a rabbit is shorn, the first fleece harvested would resemble a plucked fleece with these exceptions. It would be shorter and lack the root ends of the fibers. "Second cuts" and new hairs just beginning to grow would mar the fleece with very short hairs.

Second and subsequent fleeces shorn from this rabbit will be much different. Without the stimulus of plucking, the hairs will grow and mature at different times. Early-growing guard hairs will have their tips removed with shearing so that one fleece will have the tips and the next will have the shafts. This chopping up of the integral hair structure results in a more homogeneous or even-textured fleece. Fiber length will be shorter than if the same fleece were plucked, and there will be more very short fibers present, both of which contribute to angora's infamous shedding. Without the support of intact guard hairs, the resulting fabric will not be as furry as if it were made from plucked fibers.

The age of the rabbit is another important factor in grading angora. It takes a mature rabbit to produce the length, strength, and stature of prime angora. Baby angora is usually shorter, but more importantly, finer and more cottony. It felts easily and behaves differently when knit or woven and worn. I wait until an animal is a year old before using its hair for my commercial sweaters, although you can get away with using a nine-month fleece for a personal project. Baby angora is best reserved for wool blends (using less than 30% angora) where it is used to add softness and warmth. A baby angora blend relies on the wool for strength, elasticity, and durability.

Breed Characteristics

There are also fiber differences between breeds of angora rabbits, although these may be more subtle and can vary with individual rabbits. These descriptions are generalized and you may find exceptions within each breed.

French angoras have the kind of fleece which most typifies the luxury of fashion angora. The fibers are more substantial than those of the other breeds, with a higher percentage of guard hairs. This is commonly misperceived as a disadvantage. However, it is the guard hairs which support the loft and fluff of the angora and also help reduce felting. French angora is furry, even "spiky", and the most lustrous of all angoras (except for satin angoras, which, along with jersey woollies, will not be considered here).

The hair of *English angoras* is the finest in diameter and includes the fewest number of guard hairs in the fleece. As a result, English angora fabric has a velvety aura, rather than a dramatic furriness. The fine diameter of the fibers make it somewhat more difficult to draft in spinning, and it felts more easily.

German angoras have a fleece that is halfway between the French and the English in terms of fiber diameter and percentage of guard hairs. The guard hairs on German angora rabbits develop quite late, so it is especially important with German angoras to wait for a fully mature fleece (more than one year old). As long as it is plucked, German angora produces garments nearly as furry as the French. In my own business, I use both German and French angora to give my sweaters that classic "fur" look. I reserve English angora for special uses, such as baby garments.

Fleece Color

White angora rabbits are the only true albino animals whose hair is used as a textile fiber. As pure white as a natural fiber comes, it is much whiter than creamy wool, though it lacks the brilliance of bleached cotton. Generally speaking, white angora tends to have greater length and better fleece structure than colored fibers.

While white is the predominant color in the commercial angora market, the emphasis in this country on handspinning and rabbit exhibitions has led to the development of more than a dozen natural colors. These natural pigments are deposited in the walls around the medulla and are most concentrated at the tips. Because they are embedded in the fiber, natural colors cannot fade with age, exposure to light, or washing. Also, they cannot irritate sensitive skin. Naturally colored angora typically has a shorter staple length and more guard hair. Quality is more variable because breeding emphasis has been on color rather than fiber quality.

The plethora of natural color names can be a source of confusion for the handspinner. Often the popular names—blue, lynx, lilac, opal—are more exotic than informative. Even simple names like "black" turn out to be misleading, because rabbit raisers determine the color of a rabbit by the color of the short fibers on the hair and face. The long, spinnable fleece is often a more dilute shade. Therefore, a "black" angora rabbit produces gray fiber. Due to this "dilution" factor, many different rabbit "colors" are essentially the same when you look at the long, spinnable fibers. Most are variations of fawn or gray. Specific natural colors are defined in the American Rabbits Breeders Association Guidebook. However, even with these standards, rabbit breeders in different areas of the country call the same colors by different names. To simplify matters in my business, I have limited myself to three natural colors—white, fawn, and gray (black to rabbit raisers).

Exotic colors are bred, not for the handspinner (because most are only slight variations of the standard colors), but for the promotion of show rabbits. The development of a new, exotic color becomes a selling point, not the quality of the fiber. Exotic colors often bring higher prices because they are rare. Usually a more common color will suit the handspinner's needs just as well. If you buy angora fiber by mail, ask the color of the spinnable fiber rather than the color of the rabbit. Better yet, request samples. Even if this costs a few dollars, you will better know what you are getting.

French Angora Rabbit. Note the well structured fleece with guard hair covering and lack of furnishings.

German Angora Rabbit. Notice the heavily furnished ears and face and dense fleece.

Fawn and white young French angoras.

BUYING ANGORA FIBER

Unless you own your own rabbits, angora is not generally an easy fiber to come by. Often a spinner's choices are limited. You may be tempted to buy whatever is available and plan your project around your purchase. But how can you settle for just anything, now that you know all the possibilities? With a little research and effort, you can find exactly the kind of angora you need for your project.

Probably the best source for locating angora is the newsletter of the National Angora Rabbit Breeders Club, which contains ads from rabbit breeders who sell fiber. A visit to the small-animal pavilion at a state or county fair may help you find breeders willing to sell fiber. You can also purchase angora from local fiber arts suppliers or advertisers in textile craft magazines. Purchasing directly from a breeder, rather than from a dealer, usually results in the best price for you and more profit to the breeder, and it means the fiber has suffered less handling.

Not all sellers grade their angora fiber. Some breeders do not understand the requirements of handspinners. All grades may be mixed up together and sold for the premium price. If you are not able to examine the fiber before you buy it, be sure to ask these questions: Is the angora plucked, combed, or shorn? What is the minimum staple length? How is it packaged? Angora should be packed lightly and loosely, not mashed down into tiny bags where it can become dull and matted.

If you have the opportunity and the seller will allow it, remove some of the fibers from the bag and check them for length and structure. Are the fibers intact or clipped off? Is there a good proportion of guard hairs and down? Do the fibers lie parallel to each other, or are they all tangled? Sometimes slightly felted angora can appear OK. Tease apart a lock. The fibers should slip easily. A rabbit breeder is more likely to allow you to make a thorough inspection of the fiber than is a salesperson at a fiber convention. Although it is perfectly reasonable to expect to be allowed to inspect the fiber (everyone pulls at the locks of sheep fleeces— right?), angora is delicate and a retailer could lose a lot of expensive fiber to examination. If you're not allowed to touch, at least look at the fiber through the clear plastic bag and ask questions. Once you have bought the angora, you can examine it and return it to the seller as quickly as possible if it is not the quality represented.

Prime plucked angora, which is difficult and time-consuming to harvest, is often in short supply. You should expect to pay top price for it. Grade 2 angora will sell for probably half to a third of the going retail price of grade 1. Grade 3 angora should be a real bargain, discounted 60 to 70 percent of grade 1 price. Keep in mind the specific requirements of your project. Don't expect grade 3 angora to make fine knitwear. On the other hand, you needn't pay top price for prime plucked angora if you plan to blend it with medium grade wool for a casual sweater.

Sometimes you may find carded angora roving for sale, not as a blend with other fibers, but pure 100% angora. The price is usually at least as high as for prime plucked angora and maybe more. Angora roving is easy and fast to spin, but I advise caution before you buy. Most carding machines tend to break delicate angora fiber, producing short ends and lint which shed. Yarn spun from carded roving also produces a different effect in your final project; we will explore this more in the section on yarn design. In addition, you do not know which grade of angora went into the roving. You should tease apart a section of the roving and examine the individual fibers to determine their length and structure. Unfortunately angora roving is delicate and some sellers won't even allow you to touch it, much less pull it apart. In this case, you will have to rely on the seller's word as to the quality of the angora in the roving and if the seller has bought it wholesale from someone else, she may not even know.

A spinner once sent me by mail a sample of angora she had just purchased. She'd paid the going retail price for it and was having trouble spinning it. Could I help her out? The sample she sent me was clipped angora, all of it less than 1 inch long. No wonder she couldn't spin it! In another case, I saw a knowledgeable spinner and business woman selling grade 2 angora at grade 1 prices. Her attitude when confronted was that her customers didn't know any better, were happy with what they bought, so what difference did it make?

Now, *you* know the difference.

Working with
Angora Fiber

THE FOUNDATION OF MY BUSINESS IS HANDSPUN YARN OF 100% ANGORA. therefore I'm surprised to meet spinners who are convinced angora *must* be blended with another fiber in order to make yarn. Angora blends have a beauty and value all their own, but pure angora is supremely soft and luxurious. The silky smooth fibers glide easily, softly caressing your fingers as you spin. The experience of spinning pure angora may well dampen your enthusiasm for wool, which feels rough and coarse in comparison. Angora is truly a joy to spin.

Yarn design takes into consideration not only choice of fiber, but methods of preparation and spinning as well. Once you have decided to spin 100% angora, you should evaluate the various types of fiber preparation techniques outlined below. How—*or even if*—angora is prepared before spinning greatly influences the character of the resulting yarn and garment.

FIBER PREPARATION

Most spinners are familiar with the preparation of a wool fleece. We've soaked it in our bathtubs (to the consternation of our families) and dried it on the shrubbery (to the consternation of our neighbors). We've picked it and carded it. Many of us have also picked and carded cotton. We may have tried silk reeling or flax hackling. While there are pleasures to be derived from all this preparation, most spinners are delighted to discover that *none* of the above is required for angora.

Angora may be the only natural fiber which can be drafted and spun into a smooth yarn, right from the source, without any fiber preparation. No washing. No picking. No degumming, reeling, handling, or even carding is necessary. In fact, carding these fibers may actually introduce more tangles and in general, I don't recommend it.

This is provided, of course, that you use prime, plucked angora. Clean, smooth, and slippery, these fibers were combed before plucking so that they are parallel, which with their predominantly long staple, allows controlled drafting and spinning. You will be able to spin from this fiber a yarn which is even, strong, and durable, as well as light and fluffy. It will have a long, dense halo of fluff which some people think resembles fur, and which sheds very little. In the world of fashion, this is the yarn of choice. It makes what I consider to be the ultimate angora sweater.

Of course there are many lovely angora garments besides those made from prime plucked fiber. And with some of the lower grades, you can still avoid carding, although your yarn will be less smooth and uniform.

Angora combings which are substantially free of tangles and matts can sometimes be spun without carding. The yarn can be as densely fluffy as one made from prime plucked angora. To achieve the best results, spin slowly to allow time for your fingers to separate the fibers. Guard against overtwist, which can occur if you allow the wheel to continue to turn while you untangle the fibers. Those most likely to spin combings are rabbit raisers or spinners who know rabbit raisers. These people have access to a lot of combed fiber and may find it worth the extra time it takes to make a fine, smooth yarn from it. Of course, if you prefer a textured, lumpy yarn, you can spin combings in any fashion without carding. High quality, shorn angora can be spun without any preparation, but the resulting yarn will be different than that spun from plucked fiber. Shorn angora tends to remain in locks, like shorn sheep wool, and cut ends stick together. As you spin, you must take extra care to separate the fibers. The little stuck-together cut ends protrude from the yarn in a novelty effect. The resulting garment may be attractive, but the clumped ends contribute a rough, unrefined look.

Someday you may come by some angora—perhaps even some prime plucked angora —which has compacted from being stored too long in too small a bag. If the compaction is not too serious, it can be remedied by a very gentle picking with your fingers. Separate the fibers lightly, but avoid changing their parallel arrangement as much as possible. You may be able to spin this decompacted fiber without carding. Keep your movements light and easy to avoid introducing tangles into the parallel fiber arrangement.

I am sometimes asked if angora should be prepared by worsted or woolen methods. These terms apply to commercial preparations of wool and are not particularly applicable to angora, though some similarities can be drawn. Prime plucked angora is similar to a worsted preparation because the fibers are predominantly long and parallel. It yields a strong, dense yarn which some people mistake for a blend because they are accustomed to the fragility of commercial angora.

Carded angora and commercial rovings more closely resemble woolen preparations in that the fibers are not parallel, and there is greater variation in fiber length. When angora is carded, the resulting yarn is less substantial and loftier (less dense), but not as furry. The short fibers in carded angora may shed, and texture and color are more even throughout the yarn.

Carding Angora

To spin a uniform yarn from combings or shorn angora, some type of carding is needed to separate the fibers and reduce tangles. For best results, choose hand cards or a drum carder whose card clothing has very fine, closely set teeth, ground to points which penetrate between the fibers. Card clothing must be absolutely clean. Wool grease and hay chaff will not improve the quality of your carded angora.

You may hand card angora in much the same way that you card wool, keeping in mind that angora is a much finer and more delicate fiber and should be handled accordingly. For the best results, charge the bottom card very lightly and evenly by allowing the teeth to pull fibers from your hand. Try to keep the fibers near the surface of the card clothing. Move the top card over the bottom card, without allowing the teeth to scrape. The object of this movement is to transfer fiber from the bottom card to the top card as gently as possible. When no more fiber will transfer without scraping the teeth together, strip the fibers off the bottom card and repeat the process, until the fibers are carded to your satisfaction (which depends on how textured you wish your yarn to be). Then it can be doffed and rolled lightly into a rolag. For a fine yarn, your rolags should be about the diameter of a pencil. You may choose to make two rolags after each carding, one from each card. Thicker rolags—up to one inch in diameter—are better used for textured, heavier yarns—and are not usually suitable for pure angora.

You will probably find carding angora with regular wool cards, rather than cotton or fur cards, difficult and frustrating. You may have greater success if you use only one inch of the card clothing near the bottom edge and brush extremely gently.

Whatever type of cards you use, the key factors to keep in mind are to card *very* small amounts of fiber at a time and to do it *very* gently. Overloading the cards will put more tangles into the fiber, defeating the purpose of carding.

If you are already familiar with cotton spinning, you may enjoy an angora version of the cotton *puni*. To make an angora puni, card the fiber as just described, but do not doff. Rather, place a long pencil (or a piece of finely sanded, 1/4 inch dowelling) along the edge of the teeth at the handle side of the card. With your fingers, pull up some of the fiber ends and begin wrapping them around the pencil. As soon as the fibers are held on by tension, rotate the pencil while simultaneously bringing it toward the outer edge of the card, thereby wrapping the fibers tightly around the pencil as it is removed from the card. When all the fiber is securely wrapped around the pencil, push up on the cylinder of fiber. It pops off the pencil like a spring. You now have an angora puni, ready to spin from either end. I am not partial to this method, but it does have several attractive advantages: punis are compact, they keep fiber from flying around, and are convenient to handle if you spin on a hand spindle, charka wheel or great wheel.

Drum carders have some inherent problems for handspinners regardless of the type of fiber used. Originally, drum-style carding machines were designed to card batts for quilting. In batts, the fibers are arranged in a random fashion. They are difficult—and slow—to draft from when used "whole" because too much fiber gets drawn into the orifice. Tearing batts into narrow strips pulls the fibers even more out of alignment. Roving and sliver are more appropriate for spinning. The fibers are arranged either circularly or parallel and the narrow diameter of the preparation permits rapid drafting. Unfortunately, equipment to produce roving and sliver is not readily available to handspinners. Drum-carding angora produces noils and tangles and the resulting yarn tends to have slubs and weak spots. However, drum carders are what is available, and many spinners use them. If this is your choice, use the finest card clothing you can find and charge the card clothing lightly. A light spray of spinning oil can help control the fly. It feels grimy, but washes out.

Angora roving

Many handspinners would rather spin than card, and so prefer to buy commercially prepared roving or send their fibers to a commercial carding service. For all the wool sliver, silk bricks, cotton roving, alpaca top, and carded cashmere available, it is astonishing that until recently, commercially carded 100% angora was not available to handspinners.

In 1987, a commercial roving of pure angora was developed and introduced to handspinners. It contains a high percentage of spinning oil to reduce static during carding and to produce a coherent roving. The fiber feels sticky and gummy, a little like grease wool, and the fibers do not draft as easily as unoiled angora. However, the oil washes out completely, so the finished product is soft.

I was involved in the preliminary testing of this commercial roving and was thrilled to discover that it cut my spinning time in half. Spinning from roving is *fast*. Unfortunately, I couldn't use the carded roving for the kind of garment I generally produce because, even when the roving is made from prime plucked angora, it yields a very different yarn than the uncarded fiber does.

The differences are illustrated on the next page. I made each hat from the same prime plucked angora, spun to the same gauge and knit in the same manner. The only difference is that I use carded roving to make the hat on the left and uncarded fiber for the hat on the right.

Notice that the first hat has downy fluff, rather than dense fur. The black, silver, and gray color variations that are noticeable in the second hat are blended into a homogeneous gray in the first one.

Variations in texture are also reduced. Not apparent from the photograph are the lighter, loftier quality of the yarn and the short, fine fibers which fall freely from it. Clearly the carding process has made some substantial changes in the character of the finished product.

Some of these changes are due to the mechanical carding which apparently damages and breaks some fibers. The result is angora "lint" and short fibers which shed easily. The furry halo does not develop because the fibers are shortened by

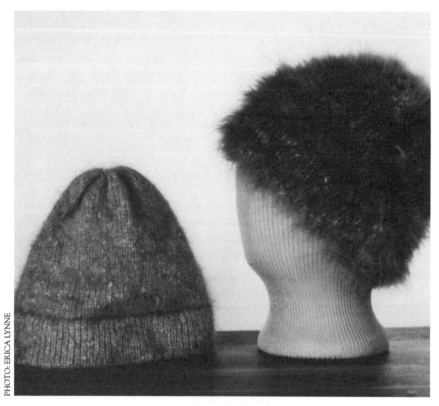

PHOTO: ERICA LYNNE

Both hats were knit and spun from the same 100% grade 1 angora. The hat on the right was spun from uncarded fiber. Angora fiber for the hat on the left went through a commercial carding machine especially for angora fiber.

this breakage and the non-parallel arrangement of the fibers traps greater lengths of the fiber within the matrix of the yarn. Color blending is to be expected when carding. However, the results are more dramatic for angora because the pale root ends are more visible in the carded preparation. In yarn spun from uncarded, plucked angora, these nearly colorless ends tend to stay hidden in the core, while the deeply colored tips display themselves on the surface.

With the exception of its greater tendency to shed, yarn spun from commercial roving is satisfactory for many handspun projects. Some people prefer the loftier (but not furrier) yarn and more demure appearance. It is well suited to decorous women's apparel, infants' clothing, or any project where the softness of angora is desired without the flamboyant furriness.

Your choice of fiber preparation—or lack of it—depends on a variety of interrelated factors: aesthetic preferences, personal sense of fashion, convenience, economy, and the availability of equipment and fiber. Whatever method you choose, obtaining and preparing sufficient fiber for your end product before beginning to spin makes for more consistent results and more efficient spinning.

SPINNING ANGORA

Angora hasn't a handspinning heritage comparable to that of cotton, wool, silk, or flax. Experts in other fibers can regale you with tales of women in the mountains of Greece spinning on handspindles while their husbands make ewe's milk cheese, or of Gandhi spinning cotton—a casteless occupation—on a charka wheel in India. By the time angora was introduced in Europe as a textile fiber, the flyer wheel and even a healthy textile industry were already well established. I am forced by history to stick to the nuts and bolts aspects of making angora yarn.

The technical aspects of spinning are not difficult to understand. Far from taking the joy out of spinning, I have found that technical mastery gives me great satisfaction by allowing me to realize a broader range of possibilities. I spend less time worrying about uncertain—possibly poor—results and more time spinning. Gauge (grist or diameter) and twist are the two primary factors in yarn design.

My first efforts at spinning angora were nothing to write home about. For one thing, operating under some misguided principle of economy, I sold my best fiber and spun up the worst. Second, I spun these ragged, matted fibers just as I'd been spinning wool. The thick, heavy yarn hung in limp, lifeless skeins. I didn't know it then, but my error was in gauge, or grist.

Angora, for all its wonderful warmth and softness, does not have the elasticity of wool. Having no crimp and springiness, a large-diameter angora yarn sags under its own weight. (Happily, an angora fabric doesn't need to be thick to be light and warm.) Since my early experience, I have designed three pure angora yarns which I use routinely in my business. You are by no means limited to these gauges. I describe them here so you can get an idea of the effect of gauge on pure angora yarn.

The first is a weighty, opulent two-ply yarn of 55 yards per ounce. In my experience, this is as heavy as angora can be spun without sagging. This yarn is ideal for knitting the fanciest adult apparel in a fabric that resembles a sumptuous fur.

The next yarn, a finer two-ply, is light and airy, perfect for delicate shawls, lacy camisoles, and infants' clothing. Strong enough for warp, it measures 110 yards per ounce. This is far from the finest gauge to which angora can be spun. The only

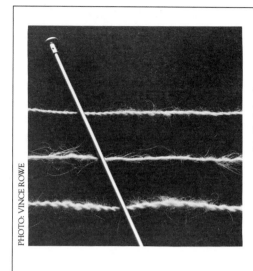

PHOTO: VINCE ROWE

Three versatile angora yarns:
2-ply, 100–110 yd/oz;
single, 100–110 yd/oz; and
2-ply, 55 yd/oz.

practical limit to how fine angora yarn can be is your ability to spin fine yarns. Angora is more difficult to spin exceedingly fine than wool because of its smoothness and lack of crimp; using a long staple (3 to 4 inches) will help. The increased surface area of the longer fibers increased the friction. I'd love to see the fine spinners—the record holders—try their hand at angora.

I use a two-ply yarn in most projects. Plying adds strength and, more importantly, elasticity to yarn. Pure angora benefits from any techniques which increase elasticity, especially when used in knitting. A three-ply yarn adds even more body. The results are exquisite if you have the time to spin the extra length and can spin finely enough to keep the final yarn gauge small. I don't find 100% angora singles strong enough for knitting alone or for warping, although I have known spinners to use angora singles, at least in knitting. I once successfully used an angora/silk blend single-ply in a warp, but it did fray apart in several places. I can't really recommend it.

A single ply of angora works wonderfully when knit together with other yarns though, and makes a feathery soft weft yarn. My single-ply angora yarn is spun at 100 yards per ounce. Single-ply angora, especially for use as weft, is a little tricky to spin because you have to spin it tightly enough to hold together, but not so tightly that it kinks up. Even if you never stop to count the twists per inch in your yarn, nor measure the slant, you'll have greater success designing yarn if you at least consider some basic principles of twist. It is, after all, what holds the yarn together.

Twist keeps the fibers in a yarn in close enough proximity to each other that friction can hold them together. There must be enough twist to produce a coherent yarn. More twist will add greater strength, but too much twist will contort the fibers and possibly break the yarn. (Spinners see this most often when twist builds up in a thin spot in the yarn. The fibers kink up and break.) Deciding how much twist to put in your yarn is an important design factor. You can do it yourself, or you can let the wheel and the fiber do it for you. If you want to do it yourself, consciously, how do you decide how much twist to put in?

In general a heavier yarn needs less twist than a fine one, because the larger number of fibers in the heavy yarn provide more friction. A yarn with little twist feels softer than one with a lot. This is how relatively soft wool garments are made from long, coarse wools—the yarn is spun with a large diameter and as little twist as possible. The converse is also true. You can ruin the softest cashmere by putting in so much twist that the yarn becomes unpleasantly hard. A high twist yarn is stronger than one with low twist (up to the point that the fiber is actually damaged by excess twist and kinking). Usually, a high twist yarn is smoother than a low twist yarn because the extra friction keeps the fiber under control. However, angora is so fluffy that this need not be a major concern. If all this seems confusing, return to your vision of your final project and keep that firmly in mind as you make your decisions. It is the results that you want to see that determine your design choices.

For general guidelines, you may consider the following information on twist in pure angora yarns. My heaviest yarn has 4 to 5 twists per inch (t.p.i.) in the singles and is plied at 2 t.p.i. The finer plied yarn has 8 to 9 t.p.i. in the singles and 4 in the ply respectively. The single-ply yarn has less twist, about 3 t.p.i.

These figures are for yarn spun from prime plucked angora. For carded fiber, the twist can be reduced because the irregular fiber arrangement provides more friction than the parallel arrangement of the plucked fiber. Commercial angora yarn, which is spun with the minimum amount of twist possible, is as low as 1 t.p.i.

Regulating the gauge and the amount of twist in your yarn requires considerable control. It helps to get all your fiber from one source and prepare it all before you begin to spin. It also helps to display a yarn sample at the correct gauge, under tension, where you can see it to duplicate the size as you spin. Finally, keep in mind that the gauge of the yarn is determined by the amount of fiber you allow to enter the drafting zone. Attempts to decrease yarn diameter by overtwisting are defeated when the tension is released and the fibers relax. This effect is even more pronounced with angora fibers because of their smoothness and inelasticity.

Spinning Equipment

Most handspinners in the United States spin on some sort of flyer wheel, and for most people, this is the fastest and easiest type of wheel for spinning angora. My personal choice is the "Nonpareil" built by Norman Hall of Oxford, New York, a handsome oak wheel with well-balanced drive wheel and smooth teflon bearings. It also has a high wheel-to-whorl ratio that is adjustable, and an efficient "heel-toe" treadle action. I sometimes spin as much as seven hours a day, so facility and efficiency are of utmost importance to me.

You don't need the world's best wheel to spin angora, though; most flyer wheels will work quite well. Some wheels, both antique and modern, have a take-up speed which is too fast for angora, especially for beginners. I can recall without affection an antique flax wheel which whisked the fibers from my fingers time after time. If you have not yet purchased a wheel and think you will want to spin angora often, you might consider trying to spin on several models and rejecting any you consider too fast. Do not despair if you already own a wheel with fast take-up. Here are some simple adjustments which will allow you to spin angora.

Yarn take-up decreases as the amount of yarn on the bobbin increases. Use this principle to reduce the take-up on your wheel by starting to spin angora on a bobbin which is already half full of clean, fine yarn. Or increase the diameter of the bobbin shaft by attaching a cylinder of foam rubber. Another way to slow the take-up is to loop the yarn over an additional hook—one on the opposite side of the flyer from the hook you are using to guide the yarn onto the bobbin.

There is no problem of take-up with a great wheel or other spindle-type wheels, because you alternate spinning with winding the yarn onto the spindle. This also allows for more accurate control of the amount of twist in the yarn. An accomplished great-wheel spinner can produce yarn as quickly and efficiently as flyer-wheel spinner. However, drafting is more difficult on the great wheel because it must be done with just one hand (usually the left, while the right hand controls the turning of the wheel). For this reason, unless you are already comfortable spinning on a great wheel, I do not recommend you try it for angora. (Because of the single handed drafting, you will probably have greater success spinning with rolags than from uncarded plucked fiber.)

The oldest and simplest spinning tool is the handspindle. It is commonly used in pre-industrial cultures where it is considered more efficient than spinning wheels, not because it is faster (it isn't) but because it is small and portable and yarn can be spun anytime the hands aren't employed in other activities. Modern spinners may find handspindles useful for similar reasons. They travel easily and can be used for some demonstrations where a bulky wheel would be impractical. A light weight, well-balanced hand spindle is the best choice for spinning angora.

You'll probably find rolags easier to manage than uncarded fiber. As with the great wheel, spinning angora on a handspindle is more difficult than on a flyer wheel and you probably want to do it only if you are already an accomplished handspindle spinner.

Spinning Hints

Angora fibers are not fluffy when first spun. The ends will slip out later, without brushing, as you knit or weave. Loosen the tension on your wheel as much as possible and spin from your rolag, roving, or the root ends of the plucked fiber. (It is more difficult to spin from the tips, some of which are stiff and hard.) Handle the fibers lightly and gently.

Correctly formed joins are especially important when working with angora because the fiber is smoother and more slippery than wool. Always join unspun fiber to unspun fiber; do not attempt to join unspun fiber to spun fiber, or spun fiber to spun fiber. You will certainly create weak spots. There should always be enough unspun fiber on each side of the join so that the integration of the fibers is complete. For a leader thread on your wheel, I recommend a clean wool yarn, with unspun fiber at the end.

One other thing to consider when spinning angora is the buildup on the bobbin. This angora yarn may be finer than you are used to handling, and fine yarns require frequent hook changes for the buildup to be regular. A smooth, regular buildup will avoid tangles when you are unreeling the bobbin. A bobbin full of tangled, frizzy angora singles, produced after hours of ultra-fine spinning, is a disaster I wouldn't wish on anyone. When spinning angora, you will probably adapt the spinning method you are most comfortable with. I use neither a long nor a short draw. I've found that Allen Fannin's technique, described in his book, *Handspinning: Art and Technique*, to be fast and efficient. With this technique, spinning is nearly continuous. The drafting occurs between the two hands: one hand holds the fiber supply and the other hand draws out the fiber while simultaneously rolling the fiber so as not to impede the twist. The wheel take-up is adjusted to just match the drafting speed. The yarn is produced smoothly, continuously, and rapidly, with a minimum of hand movement.

Finishing Your Yarn

Setting the twist is optional for a two-ply angora yarn with a balanced twist. (If your yarn is irregularly spun or plied, you may benefit from setting the twist.) I rarely, if ever, do it. Angora is so clean the yarn does not even need to be washed before use.

I do recommend setting the twist on angora singles which will not be knit or plied with other yarns. I wash the yarn before setting the twist, because it is easier to wet the angora with the addition of soap or detergent. Angora is notoriously difficult to wet thoroughly. After rinsing, the yarn should be allowed to dry slowly under tension. There should be only enough tension so that the yarn lies flat without kinks, and the tension should be removed the minute the yarn is dry (or even before it is completely dry). Too much tension will damage what little elasticity angora has. Angora yarn stressed by too much tension will become dull and lifeless.

On occasion, I've been in a real hurry to use angora singles. I have had good results setting the twist quickly by winding the yarn onto a yarn blocker—or even a skein winder—under light tension and then spraying the yarn with warm water (from the nozzle of a well scrubbed Windex bottle). The yarn dries more quickly than if thoroughly wetted and seems relaxed enough for most uses.

Controlling the Fluff

There is one other problem, characteristic of angora, which affects not the yarn, but the spinner and her environment. The light, fine angora fibers fly away easily and cling to everything. In short, spinning angora can be messy. Over the years, I've learned a few tips which help keep the fiber contained.

When spinning angora, it helps enormously to cover your lap with a generous piece of material which is reserved solely for that purpose. (Do not use an apron, unless you leave the strings untied for rapid exit.) This will keep the majority of the fiber off your clothes. Fluff attached to your clothing is a major source of fiber dissemination throughout your house. If you have to get up suddenly—to answer the phone, or rescue a crying child—quickly fold the cloth over once or twice (depending on how much time you have). This traps inside any unspun fiber. The folded cloth can be placed aside while you attend to other business and then unfolded later to resume spinning. The point is to keep all the fiber in one place, which is to say, near your spinning wheel. Any fibers which do manage to get on your clothes can be removed with a clothes brush. Keep one handy near your wheel and use it before you leave the area.

Of course it goes without saying that you don't spin angora in the kitchen, and also that you make every effort to keep the fiber away from unattended pets and small children, who, I am told, find the fiber highly entertaining.

BEAUTIFUL BLENDS

Like a child in a candy store, I'm overwhelmed at the vast array of fibers available to handspinners today. Silks—soft and lustrous as moonbeams. Superfine Merino. Clouds of kid mohair. Bundles of camel down. Cashmere. Qiviut. I try to conceive ideas, plan a project, generate reasonable purchasing goals, but the temptation of all those luscious fibers is too much. Unable to decide, I go home with dozens of one-ounce packets. A mounting collection of these assorted fibers introduced me to fiber blends—because the single rational question which penetrated the haze of my fiber intoxication was: How will this work with angora?

Angora adds softness, texture and romance to yarns made with more ordinary fibers. In turn, other fibers can complement and enhance the beauty and utility of angora.

Some spinners use other fibers to "stretch" angora. Before blending angora for economic reasons, consider the time you will spend designing, carding, spinning, and knitting or weaving, as well as finishing. Compared to your enormous investment in time (worth hundreds of dollars), the actual purchase price of the fiber becomes less significant. If you're going to devote all that time you may as well get exactly what you want. It seems false economy to me if money is the *only* reason for blending.

Regardless of which fibers you choose to blend with angora, blending creates a whole host of new variables when you design your yarn. How many types of fiber will you blend together, how thoroughly, and in what proportions? What grade of angora will you use? What carding methods will you use? What about plying?

Before giving my first major workshop on angora, I had a fairly informal attitude towards blending—a little here, a little there—put it on the cards and see what comes out. Somehow that didn't seem worth the price of the workshop, so I set out to do a series of formal samples to study the effects of different percentages of angora in blends.

I spun one-ounce samples of 25%, 50% and 75% blends of angora with wool, *Bombyx mori* silk, alpaca top, mohair, Samoyed, and cotton. You are not limited to these specific blends, but a discussion of their characteristics will provide you with a base line for your own blending. These samples were made with first-quality fibers and thorough carding. The effects of fiber grades and degree of blending will be considered later.

Fibers differ enormously in density and this is an important factor to consider when choosing how much of each fiber to use in your blends. Silk, mohair, and alpaca are quite dense, meaning that a small volume weighs a lot. Fibers like angora, cashmere, and Samoyed are much less dense and it takes a whole pile of these fibers to equal the weight of a small volume of the denser fibers. Wool seems to fall somewhere in between. Many blend by volume rather than weight, so their blends have a much lower percentage by weight of the "lighter" (less dense) fiber. A 50-50 blend by volume of angora and wool is really closer to 25% angora and 75% wool by weight. Be aware that, if you plan to sell your products, federal labelling regulations require that you figure fiber content percentages *by weight*. In the following discussion, percentages refer to weight rather than volume.

The fluffiness of angora rises to the surface of a fabric, so a little goes a long way. The more guard hairs in the fleece, the more pronounced the visual effect of the angora will be on the fabric. The addition of only 25% angora to another fiber adds a large measure of softness and some texture while retaining most of the characteristics of the main fiber. Whether wool, silk, or alpaca, the yarn looks pretty much like itself, though a little fluffier (especially silk, which is so smooth). But when you feel it, you know instantly that something is different, because it is so soft. And just 25% angora adds a lot of warmth to even a light-weight sweater. This is an excellent way to add warmth without adding weight.

The opposite effect occurs when you spin yarn from a blend of 75% angora with 25% of another fiber. On casual observation, the yarn could easily be mistaken for pure angora. A closer examination reveals the extra springiness and strength of the wool, or the luster of silk or mohair. The addition of 25% Samoyed hides the dog hair to all but the closest scrutiny, adds strength, and is more economical if you have access to free dog hair.

Angora blended equally with another fiber results in a marvelous union of the characteristics of both fibers. Angora's fluffiness dominates: a 50% blend is *definitely* angora. At the same time, the complementary fiber contributes its own characteristics—elasticity, strength, luster.

You can, of course, do your blending by guess and by golly, but you won't always like the results, you may not be able to reproduce the results if you do like them, and you will not know the fiber composition required for labeling should you want to sell your yarn or finished projects. If you don't have a scale which weighs small amounts accurately, an inexpensive diet scale in ounces will suffice to give you a general idea (not good enough for sales, however). For large quantities, you can use the same scale you use for wool.

Fiber Quality in Blends

Lower grades of angora are often used in blends and, in fact, this is a good way to use up angora which is not good enough to be spun by itself. However, keep in mind that the quality of the angora you use will influence the quality of your yarn and you should consider the effect of the grade of angora on the design of your yarn.

The ultimate extravagance is to use prime plucked angora in your blend. This is the grade to use when everything has to be perfect—a heavenly fantasy. The use of this grade produces a yarn which will fluff up the most per ounce of angora added. Even a 25% blend will add a velvety finish to the fabric. Prime plucked angora is a good choice if your project will contain at least 75% angora, because the length will add durability and strength. You can use up to 50% of the best long staple (at least 2½ inch) clipped angora in blends with results nearly indistinguishable from that of prime plucked angora.

Good quality clipped angora or combings perform well in blends and are less expensive than prime grades. If unmatted and sufficiently long, these fibers will add most of the best qualities of angora to your yarns. The fibers blend easily and gracefully and draft smoothly so that a fine, even yarn may be spun. Using up to 50% angora in this type of blend will give a luxurious effect, though it will not be quite as dramatically fluffy as if you'd used prime plucked angora.

A tweedy, variegated yarn that knits up handsomely can be spun from combings, noils, and shorter clips. Blended with wool, this slubby, noily yarn knits up into a soft, strong, utilitarian sweater with homespun appeal. The angora "fuzz" gives a misty appearance. Natural grays are popular with men as well as women, or dye the yarn a bright color for a fashionable look. You can use up to about 35% of these lower grades of angora to spin a tweedy, noily yarn.

Carding Blends

When I hear spinners discuss carding methods, the reasons they expound for choosing one method over another seem to have more to do with expense, convenience, and availability than with the type of yarn they want to spin. After obtaining some surprising effects, I finally learned that different carding methods yield different results and that these differences can be exploited in the design of yarn.

Early in my career, I sold angora fiber and blends to handspinners. Most of my carding was done on a large industrial carding machine which blended the fibers into a splendidly carded web of gossamer fiber. At that point I didn't understand the differences between various types of carding machines and later took another batch of fibers to a carding operation that was closer to my farm, expecting the same results. I was amazed to discover that this smaller cottage-type carding machine turned out a slubby, noily batt that was more difficult to draft. I persuaded the proprietor to put the fiber through the machine again, but the angora just noiled up more. The unevenly blended noily fiber batt wasn't suitable for a fine even yarn, but I salvaged this fiber blend by changing its end use. It was quite satisfactory for an unevenly-spun tweedy yarn. It was an important lesson in yarn design.

Hand cards provide the most flexibility in fiber preparation of angora blends, because *you* control the exact amount of fiber and the degree to which it is blended. Hand cards must be used for small quantities of fibers (generally under 2½ to 5 pounds) and for blends containing a lot of angora (usually over 50%), neither of which can usually be handled by a commercial carding machine. Most fibers blended with angora are also fine, so carding equipment and general guidelines as discussed earlier should be used.

I have found it helpful to weigh out small amounts of each of the clean fibers that I want to blend in the chosen proportions, and then mix these smaller amounts before placing them on the cards. For a thorough blend, charge the card thinly and evenly. Alternate dabs of fibers for an uneven blend. After all the fiber has been carded once, I break rolags into halves or thirds and combine them randomly with sections from other rolags and recard. I repeat this process until I have achieved the degree of blending that I want.

Remember to keep the total amount of fiber on the card at one time very small. If your blend contains wool you may find that charging the card first with a very thin layer of·wool helps keep the fibers on the surface of the teeth, where the carding action takes place.

Carding on a drum carder is done in a similar manner, again following the guidelines given on pages 37–39. However, you will not be able to achieve as thorough a blending as with hand cards.

For large quantities of angora blends you can use a commercial carding service. Most such services will card angora blends, although some limit the percent of angora in the blend and some charge extra for "exotic" blends. Commercial carding machines require extremely clean fibers. This poses no problem with angora, which is naturally grease-free. But the fine wools often blended with angora are notoriously greasy and difficult to scour clean. If the fine wools are not scoured enough, the machine will twist everything into a gnarly mess, which will please neither you nor the carding machine owner. It is a good idea to consult with the carding company about the capabilities of its machine before you send your fiber.

To prepare for commercial carding, weigh out the appropriate amounts of clean fiber and then mix them together. I pull apart the fibers by the handful and toss them into an enormous cardboard box. I alternate fiber types as I add them to the box and stir them thoroughly. Once they're mixed up, you can pack the fibers tightly to ship or carry to the commercial carding machine. However, most spinners prefer that the fiber not be compacted after carding, so make sure you have large plastic bags and boxes to bring it home.

The small cottage-type commercial carding machines produce lofty batts. They have greater capacity than a hand-turned drum carder, but no greater carding capability. The fiber gets carded at just one point and then out it goes. Even with exceedingly thorough picking and mixing, the fibers won't be thoroughly blended after one carding. (Keep in mind that this refers to angora blends. These carding machines may blend other fibers quite well.) However, if you have in mind slubby yarn with bits and lumps of unblended fiber, than this is the operation for you. One pass through the carding machine and you have lofty batts with uneven lumps and interesting streaks of angora.

For a complete union of fibers, the large industrial carding machines work best. They card and doff the fiber several times for a more complete blend. The thoroughly blended, well-carded fiber drafts easily—ideal for fine, uniform yarns.

The degree to which you plan to blend your fibers is inextricably bound into your decisions on the grades of angora and the method and equipment for carding. Your options range from a yarn spun from a complete union of two or more fibers with combined characteristics of the indistinguishable components, to a yarn displaying the individual characteristics of each distinct fiber. For the former, use the best grade of angora and thorough hand carding or industrial carding. For the latter type of yarn, choose lower grades of angora and uneven handcarding, drum carding, or carding on a cottage-type carding machine.

Other Blending Methods

Plying yarns of different fibers allows for maximum individuality of each type. You can make attractive yarns by plying together angora, silk, and/or wool singles. The different fibers lend their characteristics to the yarn, but behave independently. For example, a single strand of angora plied with a single strand of wool does not have the elasticity and resiliency of a 50-50 blend of angora and wool; the angora's fluffiness and the wool's resilience are segregated rather than distributed throughout the yarn. The effects are interesting, but this technique should be used with care. It's easy enough to ply together a small sample to see if this sort of yarn is suitable for your project.

Commercially carded angora blends in a variety of ready-to-spin combinations are available. These blends are typically expensive, but they can still be worthwhile if carded from high quality fibers (especially if you don't much like doing your own fiber preparation). Of course, any time you use prepared roving you sacrifice some of your own design potential. Even so, you can retrieve much of it by using the information in this chapter to assess the fiber preparations available and their suitability to your design.

Design Factors

Once you start working with blends, fiber choices may dominate your design decisions. But keep in mind the principles of gauge and twist discussed earlier, because these factors will continue to exert a strong influence on your yarn. The dominant fiber in your blend will largely determine your spinning technique and method of setting the twist.

For most purposes, protein fibers blend well with angora, the plant fibers are not so suitable (the "animal to animal and vegetable to vegetable" rule). Also, the length and diameter of the other fibers should be similar to those of angora because different fibers tend to make better blends if their respective fiber lengths and diameters are similar. When fiber lengths are radically different, the carding action favors the longer fiber. The shorter fibers tend to segregate rather than blend with the longer fibers and don't get carded. (Of course, you could use this factor to produce interesting design results as well.)

The most suitable fibers to blend with angora are those which complement its special character, elasticity and strength, or modify it for greater functionality or a less feminine look. For example, if blending with wool for a knitting project, a spinner would want to choose a fine, soft wool (to match the softness of angora) and a lot of crimp (which would add elasticity). Blending angora with a long-staple, coarse wool, on the other hand, might add strength, but not elasticity, and the two fibers would antagonize each other (soft and fine vs. coarse). However, you must make your own decisions based on your projects and goals. I know of one individual who blended her own angora with flax tow from another project. Not a blend that I would choose, but she was an angora rabbit who was making a nest for her babies. I guess it provided the right combination of softness and strength. (She'd pulled the flax tow into her cage from a nearby table where it had been left by a spinner.)

Blending With Wool

Perhaps the fiber most often blended with angora is wool. Individual preferences aside, wool is undoubtedly the most versatile and useful of all textile fibers. It is comfortable and warm even when wet. Its resilience allows it to hold its shape well, drape gracefully, and resist wrinkling. Wool can be soft enough to cuddle a baby or durable enough for carpeting. If I were stranded on a deserted island with only one fiber to choose, there's no doubt is would be wool.

Superfine fleeces like those from Merino sheep are ideal for blending with angora. My current passion is an ultrafine type of Merino called Sharlea. Sharlea sheep are given specially calculated nutritional feeds and are raised indoors with a protective cover over their fleeces. Their wool is graded for fineness and quality before it is sold. Ultrafine Sharlea fibers are about 16 microns in diameter—comparable to the fineness of angora. The staple length is 2¼ to 4 inches long—an ideal length for blending with prime plucked angora.

Clean carded Sharlea is as expensive as prime plucked angora, so blending isn't for economic reasons. The crimp and resilience of the wool will help any garment made from this blend hold its shape and drape beautifully, but the fineness and softness of the Sharlea won't detract in any way from the softness of the angora.

Regular Merino fleece averages about 20 microns in diameter, is nearly as nice as Sharlea, and is less expensive. Merino adds a subtle "silvery" luster to a blended yarn. A 50-50 blend of Merino and prime plucked angora makes a two-ply yarn that is light, white, and airy. Although it is 50% wool, the angora dominates the yarn, and a garment knit from this blend is often perceived as being pure angora. Using the same quality fibers, you can reduce the angora content to 25% and still have a lovely and fluffy yarn.

Many spinners find fine wools difficult to spin. Once familiar with spinning pure angora, the fine wools seem much more approachable. The main difference in handling between fine wools and angora is that angora is slippery and greaseless, while fine wools are sticky and greasy. *Extremely* thorough scouring is necessary. Use very hot water and a strong neutral detergent like Joy. You may have to wash the fleece several times. It will not matt up so long as you do not agitate the fleece. For a perfectly thorough blend and even, uniform yarn, you will probably have to card by hand. As with pure angora, you will need cards with fine, closely set teeth. Some large industrial machines may be able to card this blend if you have extremely clean fleece and long staple angora (3 inches or more).

It you don't want to scour a Merino fleece, you could purchase Merino top for your blending. This will be more expensive, of course, but will save a lot of messy work. Pull, don't cut, the Merino top into sections by the handful to mix with angora, using the guidelines presented earlier in the chapter.

Spin Merino/angora as uniformly as possible for the most elegant results. I prefer a fine gauge (about 100 yards per ounce), but the elasticity of the Merino allows you to spin a much heavier yarn and still have a garment which will keep its shape and look attractive. This blend makes a lovely knitting yarn, perfect for dressy sweaters which can be ornamented with seed pearls and lace. It is too springy for most weaving projects.

Although not well-suited for dressy wear, medium grade wools can be blended with angora for fashionable men's wear and for warm, functional sweaters. Even when you use a medium grade wool, your yarn will benefit from your selecting a fleece of the same length as your angora fibers, and with as much crimp (for a knitting yarn) and softness of hand as possible. You would choose, for example, the crimpier, softer shoulder and brisket wool over the longer, straighter flank wool. For a weaving yarn a spinner should look for a relatively soft wool with less crimp.

Prime plucked angora blended with a medium grade wool makes a nice, fluffy yarn, with the fluff and softness proportional to the amount of angora in the blend. However, I prefer to save the best angora for the finest fleeces and use the lower grades of angora for medium grade wools.

My most popular blended yarn is a gray tweedy yarn composed of 25% white angora (combings, tangles, and small matts) and 75% gray medium grade wool. (Gray wool can be simulated by mixing black and white fleece together.) You can blend these fibers by hand, but this mixture is well-suited to any of the commercial carding machines. The white angora blends indistinguishably into the gray fiber blend, while little slubs and noils of white retain their integrity and add a tweedy appearance to the yarn. For a more uniform color, substitute gray angora for the white.

Spin this blend fine for a man's dressy sweater or for weaving, or make a medium weight yarn for a casual ski-type sweater. This yarn is also durable and functional enough for hats, scarves, and mittens. However, it does not have the elasticity of the fine wool blends, so take care in knitting to insure the garment will maintain its shape. Even 25% angora adds a lot of warmth and softness to a durable and functional wool yarn like this.

For a variation of the above blend I have plied two strands of the blended yarn with a single strand of pure gray angora yarn spun from commercially prepared roving. This beautiful three-ply yarn has extra body (due to the extra ply) and a lot of extra softness and warmth (from the angora). However, it is not demonstrably fluffy (because the commercial roving tends not to fluff up as much), and therefore retains a conservative look. The roving is so fast to spin that the extra ply isn't all that time-consuming. The slate gray of the angora roving forms a heathery effect with the charcoal gray of the fleece. This yarn, blended by both carding and plying, makes wonderful men's wear and casual clothing.

Blending With Silk

Silk is my next favorite fiber for blending with angora. Softness, length, strength, and luster are the qualities silk adds to angora without detracting from its softness. Silk's smoothness interferes very little with the downy halo of angora. But since it does not add any elasticity to the yarn, silk and angora blend must be used cautiously in knitting. (A knitting yarn of silk and angora might well benefit from the addition of a little fine wool.) Silk/angora yarns are excellent for weaving and are suitable for warp.

Silk comes in a variety of forms suitable for blending with angora. Bricks, sliver, and roving are all excellent. These combed preparations have relatively short staples for silk and should be used with long staple angora to approach as nearly as possible similar fiber lengths. Before blending, these silks must be separated by pulling off hanks of fiber. (Do not cut the silk). *Bombyx mori* silk is near white and tussah silk is honey colored. Either may be used, depending on your color preferences. For color matching: *Bombyx mori* silk and white angora, and tussah silk with fawn angora, but don't rule out color contrasts. I've made an interesting novelty yarn combining pure white angora singles plied with golden tussah singles.

Carded silk noil is generally less expensive, but it does not have as much luster as combed silk. The noils add a tweedy appearance which doesn't go well with prime angora. In my opinion, silk noil works best in a three-way blend with a medium grade wool and angora combings. In such a blend, the effects of the silk and angora are additive, so you may need as little as 12% of each to make a noticeable effect on the yarn.

Thrown raw silk waste is first quality silk which has become tangled or broken during processing. Color-coded with ephemeral dyes and stiff with gum, it seems an unlikely prospect for an angora blend. However, thrown raw silk waste can be had for less than a fourth of the cost of most prime silks and can be transformed into white, soft, shimmering fiber by degumming. Specific directions for degumming usually accompany the package. Basically it involves simmering the silk in soapy water for about an hour, and if you've done any dyeing, you can certainly degum silk. I do recommend eliminating the deeply dyed fibers from your package—especially the magentas and reds—as they tend to retain the dye. After degumming, cut the fibers into approximately 3 inch lengths and card with angora or in a blend with angora and fine wool.

It is not uncommon for spinners to dislike fiber preparation and I confess to some degree of impatience with the process myself. Occasionally the beauty of the fibers overwhelms everything else and it is a joy just to feel and work with them. This was my experience with a particularly sumptuous blend. I can still recall the mounds of fibers: the pure white fluff of angora, puffs of creamy unbleached wool, and the silver luster of silk (in this case, degummed thrown waste). There were about five pounds all together, the fibers in equal proportions, a voluminous cloud of airy shades of white. It was so much fun just looking at it that I could scarcely bear to let it go through the carding machine. Luckily, the blended fibers were gorgeous as well—the wool and angora mixed thoroughly with random streaks of silk. From it I spun a medium weight yarn which knit up handsomely.

Other Blends

Wool and silk definitely are the overall favorites for angora blend, but an enterprising yarn designer can achieve many more interesting combinations and effects with a little initiative and experimentation. Some of the other fibers you might try include mohair, alpaca, Samoyed, and the down fibers (camel down, cashmere, qiviut).

Mature mohair is generally too long and coarse to blend effectively with angora, but the finest kid mohair is a good choice. Mohair is lustrous, extremely durable, and it dyes brilliantly. It adds strength, luster and some elasticity to an angora blend. Both fibers are fluffy, and the stiff mohair fibers seem to support the angora fluff the same way that the angora guard hairs do. I once knit a triangular fringed shawl from a 50-50 hand-carded blend of gray angora and mohair, which I traded for a basket handwoven of hickory roots. The shawl was soft, with the typical halo of fluff, but it had more substance and better drape than pure angora.

Of the New World camelids, alpacas have the best grade of textile fiber that is readily available. Alpacas are raised in the mountains of South America at elevations of 13,000 to 16,000 feet above sea level. Their coats of variegated fawns, grays, coffee, black, and white, hang down to the ground and are shorn yearly. The *suri* alpaca has a finer and more lustrous fleece than the *huacaya* alpaca. Like mohair, alpaca is coarser and longer than angora, but interesting blends are possible and the range of natural colors is enticing. In this country, alpaca is generally available as combed top or roving. To blend with angora, draw off fibers from the roving and card together in the desired proportions.

Other South American camelids provide textile fibers, too. Llamas are large pack animals whose fleeces are coarser and shorter than those of alpacas. However, baby llama, if available, is finer and quite suitable for blending, especially in a three-way blend with angora and fine wool. The guanaco is a smaller animal, thought to be the original ancestor from which alpacas and llamas were derived. It has a reddish brown undercoat of soft down. Vicuñas are the smallest and rarest of the New World camelids, and have the finest, softest fiber of all. Vicuñas were hunted and killed for their pelts and meat until they were nearly extinct. Now the vicuña is protected and raised domestically in Peru. Export of vicuña fiber at this time is prohibited by law. Llamas, and to a lesser degree guanacos, are raised domestically in North America, and their fleeces are becoming more available to handspinners.

Other down fibers such as cashmere (from Asian mountain goats), qiviut (from Alaskan musk oxen), and camel down are fine and relatively short staple fibers—very delicate and soft. Although light and airy, they do not fluff up like angora. In my opinion, the down fibers should be used when one wants softness but no texture, in contrast to angora, which is soft and full of texture. It seems rather a waste of these expensive specialty fibers to blend them with angora. However, I certainly wouldn't rule out these blends, especially with a fine wool and small amounts of angora. For example, a 50% base of fine wool, 10-15% angora (say English, to reduce the number of guard hairs), and the remainder a down fiber, would spin into a soft, velvety yarn.

The undercoat of the Samoyed husky resembles angora in many ways: it is soft and fluffy and warm. It is harvested off your own or a neighbor's dog by brushing. During the spring shedding, the undercoat comes out in great gobs. A Samoyed owner can collect fiber at a rate quite impressive to an angora rabbit owner. Some people complain that dog hair smells, but the odor will wash out. Samoyed fiber is not as fine nor as soft as angora. You can discern the difference by placing some of each on a bit of sensitive skin, such as the side of your neck. Devotees of both fibers tend to consider any blending of the two a waste of their favorite fiber. However, I know at least one spinner who produces prize-winning yarns from this blend. I found the samples I made quite satisfactory. If you have easy access to Samoyed fibers, you should seriously consider this alternative. Other long-haired fluffy dog fibers (from long-haired collies, golden retrievers, etc.) present interesting design possibilities as well.

In general, angora is best blended with protein fibers—the various wools and hairs and silks that I have just described. I did do one sample series of cotton blended with angora. The results were similar to blends with angora and silk noil.

What I've described is my own experience with angora blends. I have found it valuable to calculate percentages and weigh fibers and spin samples sets, but this doesn't preclude random experimentation or even reckless abandon. Occasionally I become thoroughly disgusted at the random piles of miscellaneous fibers cluttering my attic storage room. I toss all the ones I can bear to part with (or have had for more than three years) into a large bin with just enough wool to hold it all together and provide some consistency, and ship it off to be carded. The tremendous sense of satisfaction (at clearing out my storage area) is immensely rewarding, and (luckily) the yarns have even turned out beautifully.

CONSIDERING COLOR

Back in the days when spinners were devoted to natural colors, a pair of azure skeins of handspun wool won first place at the New York State Fair. There's no doubt that the yarn was worthy of the prize for the quality of its spinning, but still—how could the judge help but be drawn by such a stunning color? Color is a compelling design component. Colors evoke feelings, create moods, and project personality. People notice color first.

Angora comes in several natural colors and an albino white onto which a full palette of colors can be dyed. Color preferences are highly personal; as always, you should feel free to experiment. What follows is just a reflection of my own experiences.

All other colors aside, white is the most majestic. White angora is elegant, classic, and enduring. My customers may be attracted to displays of brilliantly dyed angora, but most often they buy white.

If white is the queen of angora colors, then black is her closest rival. By "black", I do not mean the natural color from "black" angora rabbits, which is really gray, but a deep, intense, all-consuming black. Obsidian black is like a shining jewel which speaks more of power than of purity. True black must be obtained from synthetic dyes. It is difficult, but not impossible, to dye angora such a deep dark black, and it is well worth the effort.

The natural colors of angora—the fawns, browns, silvers and grays—are lovely in their own right. A colored angora fleece is not a single shade. Fawn angora, for example is a luscious melange dominated by honey and cream and accented with camel, slate, and chestnut. Yarns and garments made from uncarded plucked angora ripple with color, resembling an exotic fur. Thorough carding blends the colors and quiets the stronger shades.

Using more than one natural color in a pure angora sweater can be tricky. It often looks as if the knitter didn't have enough of any one color to make a whole sweater. If you do use angora in a patterned sweater, I suggest using curvy intarsia patterns rather than severe geometric ones. In woven projects, use narrow stripes in the warp. Try to use patterns which allow the eye to be introduced to the color changes, look purposefully designed, and are well integrated.

White angora can be dyed a full range of colors, from deep black to delicate pastels. Simple, true colors, whether saturated or pastel, are clear enough to complement the extravagant texture and even add some luster. Bright turquoise blue, magenta, and royal purple are some of my favorites for intense colors. Emerald green and fire-engine red are also great if these are "your" colors. Bright yellow seems too brassy and harsh in pure angora, although a clear, light yellow works well. Other pastels which suit angora well are pink and ice blue. As the angora becomes diluted in fiber blends, these color guidelines lose their usefulness.

Dyeing Angora

Angora and wool are keratin-based fibers, and therefore take dyes similarly. The differences in the physical structure do require some variation in dye technique and influence the results.

In both fibers, dye binding sites are located in the cortex. The cortex makes up the bulk of wool fibers, but it is much thinner in angora. Angora often requires two or more times the amount of dye to become the same color density as wool. The more intense the color, the greater the increase in dye needed. Remember that angora dries somewhat lighter than it appears in the dyepot.

Being finer, angora is also more delicate than wool. To reduce fiber damage, minimize the amount of heat and chemical treatments whenever possible. If possible, dye angora at lower temperatures (around 180°F). Avoid simmering more than an hour, which decreases softness and loft. Carefully calculate and measure the minimum quantities of acids, mordants and other dye assists. Avoid alkalis, which damage angora. If you must use alkaline solutions, reduce or eliminate heat, which aggravates the damage. Follow alkali treatment with a 15 minute soak in a dilute acid solution (10% vinegar in water) and a clear water rinse.

The central medulla affects the way angora takes dye, because it contains hollow spaces which cannot absorb dye. The effect of the dyeless space is hardly noticeable in the fine down fibers, which have a small medulla. However, in the large guard hairs the medulla is greatly expanded, especially in the heads, where the cavity constitutes the major portion of the diameter of the fiber. All this empty space relative to the dye-absorbing surfaces of the fiber results in a reduction in color density, especially at the heads. It is these heads which slip out of the yarn to form the halo of fur which is characteristic of angora. Their relative paleness in dyed angora creates a frosty effect accentuating angora's natural aura.

Downy angora fibers have less luster than mohair and most wool, and dyed angora has a matte finish. However, the scale structure of the guard hairs is different from that of the down and makes them dye more lustrously. This adds a certain luminescence to dyed angora. The more guard hairs in your fleece, the more luster.

When you first begin to dye angora, the most obvious characteristic of the fiber is that it is extremely difficult to wet. Raw fiber and yarn float readily. Even after submersion and squeezing, the fine, fluffy fibers retain large air bubbles which are absolutely dry. These bubbles may be as large as an inch in diameter. We are not talking about uneven dyeing here. We are talking about the difference between color and pure white. These bubbles will not work their way out as you simmer the dyepot. You must get rid of them before dyeing.

Because there is a little oil on the fibers, angora will wet and dye better if you wash the skeins (or garments) thoroughly in a neutral pH detergent. (I use Joy.) After rinsing, return the skeins to a pot of warm, sudsy water and squeeze gently, working your hands over every inch of fiber. It is important not to agitate the fibers (which doesn't help wet them anyway) or treat them roughly. Both will encourage felting. Repeated firm, gentle squeezing and soaking over a period of 12 to 24 hours will insure that the angora is thoroughly wetted. Once the fiber is completely wet, you may proceed with your usual dyeing technique. Blends of angora with other fibers, especially wool, will wet much more easily. The water can travel along the other fibers, drawn by capillary action, to get in contact with the angora.

Angora is not a wash-and-wear fabric, and I am not saying that you can ignore proper handling techniques. However, angora does not deserve its reputation for easy felting, especially if you use long-staple plucked fibers. If you are used to handling wool, you will find that angora needs only a little extra care in handling. Don't agitate the fiber. Don't stir roughly. Squeeze rather than wring. Lay flat to dry. These are all rules that you should be familiar with already if you dye wool.

When angora yarn is dyed in skeins, the fluff tends to bind the individual strands of yarn together. These pull apart when dry. Unraveling the skeins will be easier if you tie them loosely with cotton thread in at least eight places for a two yard skein, preferably in the figure-8 pattern. Angora may appear matted when it is wet, but this is an illusion. When thoroughly dry, the angora will fluff up again beautifully. Take note of the care instructions beginning on page 92 for more details on handling and fluffing up angora.

Using Natural Dyes

Although you can use natural dyestuffs to dye angora, in general I have found them less than satisfactory. The unpredictability of natural dyes has the tendency to inhibit experimentation on such an expensive fiber, but angora is something that I have in abundance. In addition to my own natural dyeing done on the farm, I have taken small sample skeins of angora to my old spinning guild's dyepot-to-pass gatherings and have therefore subjected angora to a wide variety of natural dyes. These compound complex dyes, which are derived primarily from plants, have an earthy quality which goes well with wool, but is rather at odds with angora. However natural dyes are quite well suited to angora and wool blends. Many natural dyes yield neutral shades which I think are better represented by the colors grown on the rabbits themselves.

The natural dye which has consistently given me the best results on angora is indigo. It can yield palest baby blue to navy. I can also recommend natural dyestuffs which yield clear yellows or oranges. I have had good success with Queen Anne's Lace (clear yellow), *Mycena leaiana*, a mushroom which dyes clear orange, onion skins (yellow) and *Hypomyces lactifluorum*, a parasitic fungus which yields apricot. The mordant I have used in all cases is alum.

Two likely candidates, cochineal and the orchil lichen, have not yielded satisfactory results in my angora dyeing. The cochineal colors seem muddy. The alkalis needed to dye with orchil lichens cause the angora to lose life and luster.

If you want to try dyeing angora with natural dyes, there is an enormous selection of books on the topic from which you can learn basic techniques and obtain suggestions on dye sources. I have just a couple of recommendations on technique. First is to limit your mordant to the least amount possible, as these chemicals have a tendency to make the fibers harsh. Alum is safest in this respect. You must be very careful with the alkalis used in dyeing with indigo and the orchil lichens.

Many natural dyers like to simmer the dyestuffs and the yarn together. I don't recommend allowing angora to come in direct contact with the dyestuffs especially ones like leaves, flowers, and bark, which have lots of small particles. You will never get the bits of dyestuff out of the fluffy angora. If the amount of dyestuff is small, you can place it in a muslin bag and simmer it along with the angora. If large amounts of vegetable matter are needed for the dye, it is better to simmer the dyestuff until you have a strong dye liquor and then strain out the solid materials before adding the angora.

Synthetic Dyes

Any synthetic dye which works well on wool should dye angora. An exception is Procion, a dye designed for cellulose fibers, though it can be used on wool as well. However, in my experience, it does not dye angora. I use Ciba Acid dyes and National Acid dyes, which are relatively easy and safe for home use. They produce pure colors with satisfactory lightfastness. A minimum amount of acid and heat is used in the dyeing process, thereby preserving the softness of angora. Dyer Nancy Morey also reports success dyeing angora with Cushing dyes and hot water fiber reactive dyes.

Telana (formerly Lanaset) dyes are more colorfast. However, they tend to dye less brightly on angora and are more complicated to use. They require the use of several assists and concentrated acetic acid, which can cause severe burns. It is dangerous to keep around the house, especially if you have small children. Serious and professional dyers may want to use Telana dyes.

The basic dyeing procedures, special equipment, and safety precautions have been reiterated too many times to bear repeating here. If you need detailed instructions on synthetic dyeing, I recommend Linda Knutson's book, *Synthetic Dyes for Natural Fibers*.

You will probably find it more difficult to produce pastel colors on angora than brilliant ones. When trying to dye a tint, pay extra attention to the wetting procedures and those which retard the fixation of the dye. (Use a large volume of water, heat very slowly, and remove the fiber from the dyepot when adding dye and other chemicals.) Also be sure to weigh and calculate accurately the amount of dye that you need. It will be quite small. You may want to reduce that number even by half, because it is easier to add more dye than it is to bleach out excess dye.

Brilliant saturated colors are easier to obtain. You will have to use more dye than you would normally need for wool—perhaps two to four times as much—and even then, the angora tips may appear frosted.

Black presents an extra challenge. You will need at least four times the usual amount of dye. It helps to start dyeing black over natural gray yarn (though in fact, black can be dyed over any natural colored angora). Black is not true color in the same sense that blue or red are. Most of the black dyes that I have seen are based on very deep blue. Even when used in excess to dye angora, some of those lovely frosted tips remain bluish. In order to get rid of the detracting sheen, you can add a small amount of red or orange dye.

Brilliant colors can be combined in an angora garment. I dye many skeins bright colors and hang them in the studio where I can see them daily. I move the skeins into different arrangements until I at least hit on the one which is most pleasing to my eye. I especially like vertical stripes of bright colors and variable widths. Besides stripes, graceful curving patterns seem to work better than geometrical ones with the fluffy, blurred surface of an angora fabric.

Rainbow Dyeing

I have the most fun when rainbow dyeing with synthetic dyes. This spontaneous free-form style of dyeing was first developed in this country by spinner Jean Stiber, who got the basic idea from an article in *The Web* (a journal for spinners from New Zealand). This technique is especially effective on angora. Basically, rainbow dyeing consists of sprinkling several colors of dye powder onto fibers in the dyepot and *not stirring*. As the dyepot simmers, diffusion and the natural movement of the water mix some of the dyes to form a rainbow of colors. You can use this technique on angora yarns, garments, and even unspun fibers.

I would never have dreamed that angora fibers could be dyed before spinning. I am greatly indebted to Connie Cummings (for many years the secretary and newsletter editor for the National Angora Rabbit Breeders Club) for sharing this technique with me. Using Connie's method for dyeing angora fiber and Jean's rainbow dyeing, I have found a most enjoyable way of dyeing angora. It is pure fun and the colors are delightful to behold.

The most difficult part is wetting the fleece. For dyeing in the fleece, I use grade 1 angora if I am planning to spin a pure angora yarn, and other grades if blending. You must wet and presoak each handful individually in a pot of warm, soapy water. Take a small handful of angora fiber and submerge it. Squeeze and release, squeeze and release. Try to keep the fibers aligned as much as possible. Look at the fibers. You will be able to see if there are large air bubbles. They appear whitish. Keep squeezing. Repeat this process, handful by handful, until all the fiber is wetted. Although this a form of variegated dyeing, the medullated tips dilute the color enough as it is without the presence of additional white fibers. You don't want any white spots. Remember to keep your movements slow and gentle, but firm enough to squeeze out the air. Avoid any excess agitation. Don't pick at the fibers. Do not stir—only squeeze. Your best efforts will leave the fibers looking terribly matted and tangled. You will probably think that you have ruined all that lovely angora. Proceed with faith. It will turn out all right.

Use just barely enough warm water to cover the fiber. This is in direct violation of the usual dyeing rule which says that you must have lots of water to circulate around the fiber. In this case, you don't want the fiber to move around and get more tangled, and besides, this is rainbow dyeing—the epitome of variegated uneven dyeing. Next add the requisite amount of vinegar, based on the weight of the fiber and the manufacturer's instructions. Place the wetted angora in the dyepot. Now sprinkle on the dyes. I use a toothpick to handle the dyes. Some people put the dyes in salt shakers. In either case, be sure to wear rubber gloves and a filtration mask when handling powdered dyes. Dyes are reactive chemicals and are most potent in their powdered form.

You can be conservative and add only two colors, in which case you will get at least three—the third arising as the first two become mixed. For example, you sprinkle on spots of red and spots of blue. You will get red, blue and many shades of purple in between. Most dyers, myself included, usually add three related colors. My favorite combination is purple/blue/pink. Turquoise/green/yellow is another combination that works well. The yellow in this combination and the pink in the former one are dominated by the other colors in the mixture. In order to make them more prominent, you can add them to the dyepot first and let them set for five minutes or so before adding the other dyes. However, it is also a nice combination when the yellow or pink add only a touch of color. Master dyer Nancy Morey specializes in rainbow dyeing. She has been known to add as many as five different colors to a single rainbow dyepot and achieves success with some unlikely combinations. So feel free to experiment. Just make sure that the fiber is spread with the maximum amount of surface area and that you cover all the white with dye.

Now comes the hardest part. **Do not stir.** Just simmer the dyepot gently and let the colors migrate and blend as they will. If you absolutely can't resist, you may occasionally poke down a bit of floating fiber or sprinkle a little extra dye onto an area that is remaining white. However, the more you stir or diddle with the pot, the more likely that you will get mud rather than a rainbow.

After the dyepot has simmered for 30 minutes to one hour, turn off the heat, and let the dyepot sit still until it is cool enough to handle easily. Then gently drain off the dye liquor, disturbing the fiber as little as possible. Lay the fiber on screens or racks to dry. (To avoid felting, do not wash unspun angora after it is dyed. Postpone washing and rinsing until after the yarn is spun.) The fibers will appear hopelessly matted, but they aren't. If you dry your rainbow dyed angora outside, keep it out of the sun and watch out for nest-building birds and brisk winds, both of which will carry it away.

As the angora dries, you can gently tease apart some of the clumps. Do not pull hard. The wet fibers stick together tenaciously, but slide easily apart when dry. You see, it isn't matted after all! This is really the most fun of all, separating the fibers and watching the unveiling of all the marvelous colors. Keep after these clumps. A perfectly dry-on-the-outside clump may harbor dampness in the interior. After drying, the rainbow dyed angora will have to be picked and perhaps carded lightly before spinning.

You can rainbow-dye skeins of yarn with random spots of color as you did with the fleece, or you can carefully divide the skein into thirds and apply one color of dye on each third, to get a more standard variegated yarn. Neither of these techniques gives me an effect that I like once the yarn is knitted, though; so if I want to rainbow dye yarn, I dye the yarn in singles and then ply it for a more random and blended effect.

You can also rainbow dye a finished garment. This technique will perk up a sweater that just doesn't have enough sass, but it is risky because you have a lot of time invested in a garment which can be ruined in one fell swoop with a bad dye job. However, once you have developed some skill with this technique, the risks are greatly reduced and it is the most efficient way to do the dyeing because you skip all the picking and carding involved in dyeing fleece, and the skeining in dyeing yarn.

When rainbow dyeing a completed sweater, put the washed, thoroughly wetted garment in the dyepot, front side up, with just barely enough water (with the required amount of acid) to cover. Sprinkle on the dyes. Sprinkling the dyes a little here and a little there works better than large blotches of dye. You want the garment to be front side up because the dyes will be the most intense where they are originally placed. Be sure to heat the dyepot slowly and keep the temperatures to a very low simmer to avoid shrinkage. After simmering for half to three-quarters of an hour, turn the garment over. At this point you may want to add a little more dye to brighten up the colors on the back, but don't add to much or it will muddy up the colors on the front. Simmer for another half hour, cool in the pot, drain, wash and rinse and lay flat to dry—resplendent in its beautiful colors.

Dyeing Blends

The range of possibilities grows exponentially when you incorporate both color and fiber blends into your yarn design. The fibers or yarns may be dyed separately or together in the same dyepot. You should not have any trouble dyeing angora blends all in one dyepot so long as all the fibers are protein-based. This would include all the mammalian fibers and silk. There may be some slight color variations with different fibers dyed all at once due to physical characteristics, or in the case of silk, chemical differences. Except for the frosty tips, angora dyes only slightly lightly than wool, especially at lower dyepot temperatures. In a well carded blend, you will not notice any difference in color. Mohair takes colors more brilliantly, while silk fibers in the same dyepot as keratin-based fibers tend to dye lighter. This variation in color intensity can be used as a design component in your yarn. I spun up a blend of 70% lambswool, 15% angora, and 15% silk noil and dyed it a deep shade of burgundy. The silk noils dyed rose and the resulting tweedy effect was quite appealing. If you prefer a more uniform color in your silk blend you can increase the intensity of the silk color by keeping the temperature fairly low and increasing the amount of acid in the dyebath. Silk absorbs dyes better at lower temperatures than keratin-based fibers.

You can create multidimensional colors from synthetic dyes by dyeing several batches of different pure colors and then blending them together, or blending them with a white or black fleece. For my mother, who loved any shade of purple, I created a lavender blend of 75% lambswool and 25% angora for a Christmas sweater. I divided the wool into three equal parts by weight and dyed one section blue and another magenta, leaving the third section white. I carded the wool together with white angora combings to make a lavender tweed sweater accented with opalescent mother-of-pearl buttons.

One of my favorite fiber blends back when I was selling carded fibers was composed of 25% rainbow-dyed angora (usually purple/blue/pink) carded into a black wool fleece. You can use combed or clipped angora for this kind of blend. Another idea: take a blend of gray wool and gray angora and dye it deep blue. Gray wool usually has white fibers in it and these, along with the light colored roots of the gray angora, will take the dye, resulting in a gray and blue yarn. Or dye over any naturally colored pure angora. Try plying rainbow-dyed angora with a single strand of white or gray wool. I knit some charming children's mittens from single-ply angora rainbow dyed red/orange/yellow plied with natural white wool. Let your imagination run wild. Set off rainbow dyed angora in purples and blues with jet black merino. Dye several handspun yarns of the same gauge but spun from angora and other fibers in the same dyepot. Use these yarns to weave a stripy shawl of related colors. Put the pizazz of color into your angora designs.

Using Your
Angora

I ONCE ATTENDED AN EXPENSIVE TWO-DAY WORKSHOP FOR ADVANCED SPINNERS. I had been frustrated in my efforts to develop my craft past the level of simply making yarn and was eagerly anticipating new developments. The workshop leader spent quite a bit of time having all of us participants introduce ourselves and more time laboriously handing out samples of carded fiber. When we finally got to some hands-on learning, it consisted of being told to "experiment" with the samples. No guidelines were given. Few explanations were offered, beyond a discussion among participants, who were all members of the same guild and basically knew each others' opinions anyway.

Needless to say, I was disappointed. I can experiment at home, and attend guild discussions for the nominal dues charged.

Another series of workshops I attended were led by a highly opinionated textile artist. We were instructed with a fervor which bordered on fanaticism. There was clearly no doubt in this leader's mind exactly what we, as handspinners, should do and how we should go about it. Some of the participants felt that this leader was too domineering. But at least we *learned* something.

In these chapters on angora garment design and care, I would like to strike a happy medium between these two approaches. Angora is a specialty fiber, and tackling a new medium can be daunting, particularly when that medium is expensive and its care so apparently intimidating. Much of what I have learned about angora knitting and weaving has come from trial and error. I have often yearned for knowledgeable advice.

The guidelines that I use and some actual project directions are the tools I offer you for the development of your own approaches. I provide this background information to you now so that you can feel comfortable working with angora, whether you're knitting a sweater, weaving a shawl, or making some smaller angora project—as well as taking care of that project once it is done.

PURE ANGORA KNITWEAR

I wish I had a dollar for every person who has told me, "You can't make a sweater out of pure angora." It's an odd thing to hear that what you've been doing to support yourself is impossible, but it seems to be a common misconception, even among professionals in the textile industry. People have become so accustomed to cheap, insubstantial commercial yarns and to angora blended with synthetics that high quality, pure angora goods are virtually unknown.

When you make angora yarn, the spinning process twists and traps the slippery fibers into a relatively smooth yarn. Many knitters—even those who are also handspinners—are fooled by the appearance of freshly handspun angora yarn. The angora fluff grows in your lap as you knit. The gentle friction of the needles and the clothing you are wearing draws it out as you move the fabric along your knees, turning it over, pulling it in and out of your knitting bag. As exciting as it is to watch any knitting project develop, angora is even more exciting, because the yarn "grows" along with the project.

In fact, knitting is an ideal medium for 100% handspun angora yarns. Knitted fabric has the softness of rounded stitches, the elasticity of their interlocking loops, and a silky, sensuous drape. If you have never before knitted with pure handspun angora, you have a real treat in store. Careful consideration of the fiber characteristics and some thoughtful design plans can help you avoid any real disappointments or disasters. My definition of a first-quality garment assumes yarn handspun from Grade 1 angora (pure, prime, plucked fiber).

You may knit pure angora by hand or machine. Some styles and patterns are better suited to handknitting than to the machines available to the home knitter—for example, double-faced fabrics, and patterns which have increases or decreases interspersed throughout the row. Some complex stitches are nearly as time-consuming on a machine as they are by hand.

Knitting Tips

Handspun angora behaves differently from wool yarn. Angora is a slippery fiber and the stitches will slide off the needles at the least provocation. It is easy to drop stitches, and the dropped stitches do not hold their shape, but rather disappear into the fabric. With sharp eyes, strong light, and a lot of practice, you can pick up dropped stitches; but believe me, it is much easier to put a little care into avoiding them. I always secure the ends of the knitting needles with a rubber band when I put my knitting aside.

All knitting begins with a sample to determine gauge. You do not have to make too many sweaters which turn out too large or too small before you learn the time-saving value of sample knitting. In my experience, angora needs a larger gauge sample than wool. Because of its relative lack of elasticity, it stretches out, sometimes in unpredictable ways. A larger sample (at least 10 inches square) which is washed, air-dried, and fluffed up will give you the best results. For the most accurate assessment of the gauge, count the stitches (or rows) over at least 5, and preferably 7 or 8 inches, and then divide the total number of stitches (or rows) by the number of inches counted.

Gauge is absolutely essential for knitting, whether you use a pattern or not. In selecting a pattern for your angora handspun, you do not need to choose a pattern which is specifically for angora yarn. You need only choose a pattern which has the same gauge as your knitted sample.

You really don't need patterns at all. Most of my handknitting is done without patterns and once you get used to this system, it is actually easier to make exactly the style and size sweater you want than it is with a pattern.

Planning a sweater without the benefit of a pattern consists of determining the dimensions of each knitted piece (graph paper can help here) and using the gauge to calculate the number of stitches and rows needed for each piece. The formula is:

$$\text{Garment dimension in inches} \times \text{gauge (sts/in)} = \# \text{ of sts.}$$

For example, you want your sweater to be 20 inches across the chest. Your gauge, as determined by your sample, is 4 stitches to the inch.

$$20 \text{ in (garment width)} \times 4 \text{ sts/in} = 80 \text{ sts.}$$

You would cast on 80 stitches. The number of rows is calculated in the same manner. If you want to have 13 inches in between the bottom of the sweater and the underarm and your gauge is 5 rows per inch, the calculation would look like this:

$$13 \text{ in (garment length to underarm)} \times 5 \text{ rows/in} = 65 \text{ rows.}$$

You would knit 65 rows before beginning the underarm decreases. Planning sleeves, necklines and underarm seams is a little more complicated, but can be worked out in the same way, measuring each dimension in inches and converting it to stitches and rows.

You can knit angora in flat pieces or in the round. Sweaters knit in the round will have a more flowing, blousy appearance. Knitting separate backs and fronts gives more form and shaping to your garment because the seams have a stabilizing effect. Ribbing often causes trouble for angora handknitters. The angora stretches out, leaving the ribbing expanded and limp. To avoid this problem without the use of elastic threads, I knit ribbings on the smallest needles possible and decrease the number of stitches (usually by 10%). A knit 2, purl 2 ribbing draws in better than the more commonly used knit 1, purl 1 and also looks more stylish.

I include this information about knitting without patterns because many fine knitters and handspinners feel bound by commercially available patterns. I believe one of the real advantages of handspinning is being able to create your own project from start to finish. There are many attractive commercial patterns, but you don't have to be limited by them. Use the patterns as you use this book, as stepping stones to your own creations.

Machine Knitting Angora

The special characteristics of handspun yarn and the final fluffiness of the fiber contribute most heavily to the look of a handspun angora project. Therefore, it is difficult to distinguish between handknit and machine knit angora. Most of my angora sweaters are knit on a home knitting machine, which in some ways is ideal for handspun angora. These machines are most efficient at knitting large sections of stockinette. Because angora has plenty of texture already in the yarn, most angora garments will be knit in plain stockinette anyway. Being slippery and not yet fluffed up, handspun angora yarn slides easily through the various slots, orifices, and needles of a knitting machine. In fact, a knitting machine can accommodate a larger diameter yarn of 100% angora than it can of wool. Handspun angora is strong enough not to break and can be knit and unraveled even more often on a machine than by hand because the machine knitting process further compacts the yarn, rather than fluffing it up.

On the other hand, machine knitting with handspun angora is not as easy in some ways as with wool, even with handspun wool. Wool yarn sits obediently in the needles. Angora is more the unruly child. Slippery and inelastic, angora will drop stitches the moment you take your eyes away. As a consequence, it takes much longer, about twice as long, to machine knit an angora sweater than a wool one. You must move the carriage more slowly and with greater care on each and every row. Knitting in this manner will help to avoid dropped stitches and make them easier to repair if they do drop. Picking up angora stitches is much more difficult than picking up wool ones, again because the yarn is slippery and inelastic. The stitches slide out of place with amazing facility. You can use a pair of forceps to gently hold the dropped stitch up and open in order to more easily insert the transfer tool. You will also have to knot your joins, at least temporarily, because angora slips too much to hold itself in place. If you are moving the carriage slowly and carefully and are still having a lot of trouble with dropped stitches, try adding more weights and be sure that the weights are distributed evenly. I have found the weights which come with the lace carriage to be most useful with angora.

This use of weights was perhaps the most difficult thing for me to get used to in machine-knitting. Previously, the emphasis in all my textile work was to avoid any unnecessary strain on natural fibers, especially a low-elasticity fiber like angora. For years, I avoided trying machine knitting because I cringed at putting all those weights on my fine handspun yarns. As it turns out, these fears were unwarranted. You can use all the weight you need while knitting. Just avoid leaving the weights on any longer than necessary. Especially do not leave an unfinished section weighted on the machine.

Gauge samples are as necessary for machine knitting as for handknitting. Because handspun angora sometimes stretches in unpredictable fashions, I knit a very large gauge sample, often as big as the back of the sweater I plan to make. Fortunately, the machine-knit samples are quick to knit and easy to unravel. Because I do want to unravel and reuse this yarn, I do not wash it and fluff it up. Instead, I let it rest overnight, or at least a few hours, before measuring. This gives the yarn a chance to relax a little. You want to use a fairly tight gauge with handspun angora to add elasticity to the fabric, but you do not want it so tight that there is no flexibility or drape. I use a standard knitting machine, rather than a bulky, for my angora yarns. A 55 yd/oz 2-ply knits up well on gauge 10, using every other needle. Even the smallest gauge on the bulky setting seems too large. For a 110 yd/oz 2-ply I use every needle, gauge 8. For ribbings, I use the smallest gauge possible and leave off a couple of stitches at each end. (You add them back on when you change to stockinette.)

Some Design Concerns

Sweater design is largely a matter of personal preference, but when working with a specialty fiber like angora, you should consider the fiber's characteristics, warmth, texture and inelasticity.

If you live, as I do, in an energy-efficient household (the thermostat set at sub-arctic temperatures), the extra insulating capacity of angora greatly assists in the struggle against hypothermia. Under more normal circumstances, it's all too easy to create a garment too warm to wear indoors.

With a little bit of thought, several design solutions are possible to reduce overheating. Consider a cardigan, which offers the option of being worn either open or closed. If you must have a pullover, a loose, oversized style will be cooler than a snug one. A lightweight yarn and lacy pattern go a long way towards reducing the insulating capacity of a sweater. V-neck and scoop necklines are cooler than a jewel style. Use a loose cowl collar to replace a tight turtle neck. As for sleeves, they can be cap, three-quarter length—or leave them off entirely. In short: loose, light and open are the styles to keep in mind.

Another thought: Consider where and when you want to wear your sweater. Long sleeves with fluff all around the wrists would be fine for the theater or symphony, but could really get messed up eating at a fancy dinner party. Three-quarter length sleeves or short sleeves over a silk blouse can look just as elegant

PHOTO: BOB MIDGLEY

The author models her "Classic Angora" cardigan of 100% handspun angora. Notice the characteristic furry halo of French angora, here in "dappled fawn". Machine knit with hand crocheted trim.

PHOTO: BOB MIDGLEY

This sweater, titled "Sandstorm", was machine knit sideways in stripes of handspun angora, tussah, Bombyx mori silk, and commercial alpaca. Sleeves are pure handspun angora, finished in crocheted angora and trimmed with an eyelet accent and an antique lace collar. Designed, spun, and knit by the author. Instructions for this sweater appeared in Cast-On magazine, Spring, 1990.

and will leave your hands free of fluff for other activities.

Because of angora's rich texture, simple lines and plain stitches are most effective. Some people would go so far as to say that angora overpowers any other design feature that you might add. But don't let that keep you from expressing your own creative ideas. For instance, I like to knit very fine angora yarn in lacy patterns. The fluffiness does blur the stitches and state fair judges will tell you that angora is not a suitable fiber for lace patterns. Nevertheless, this diffuse laciness can make angora appear even more delicate and feminine.

Many years ago I gave my yarn to several knitters to see what design ideas they would come up with. Jean Nowak knit a beautiful angora sweater accented with cables. The cables did not stand out as they would on an Aran sweater, but they were definitely visible and added something special. This is the key point, it seems to me: Does the stitch or pattern you want to use add something special to your project? If so, then feel free to use it.

Finally, consider that angora just doesn't have the springiness and bounce of wool, nor does it quickly return to shape after being stretched. Angora is more like silk—soft, loose, and drapey. If you try to use your pure angora handspun to knit a tight, form-fitting sweater, you're likely to be disappointed, because angora doesn't have the spring to cling in the fashion these styles demand.

You may have noticed by now that this chapter hasn't told you exactly how to make an angora sweater. The goal here is to give you useful guidelines for designing your own project. If you are already an experienced textile designer, you can take off from here. If you prefer to begin with more complete directions, here is the pattern for one of my original designs, a sweater I've named Charisma. It's a waist-hugging style with plunging neckline, short sleeves and button-down front.

CHARISMA
A Handspun Sweater of Pure Angora

These directions are for size 10. Changes for sizes 12, 14, and 16 are in parentheses.
Materials:
>2-ply (100% handspun angora, gauge 55 yards/oz.)
>10 oz. (12, 14, 16)
>2 pairs straight knitting needles to achieve gauge
>1 crochet hook
>5 5/8-inch buttons

Gauge: 4 stitches = 1 in. 5 rows = 1 in. **Make a gauge sample!** I use needle sizes 3 and 5, and crochet hook E, but this is only a suggestion. My knitting is looser than average, so I usually use smaller needles than other knitters would.

Back: Using smaller needles, cast on 60 stitches (65, 69, 72). Knit 2, purl 2 in ribbing for 3¼ inches. Change to larger needles, and work in stockinette. In the first row, increase 1 stitch in the first stitch and evenly space 7 (6, 6, 7) more increases across the row. Knit even in stockinette until the piece reaches 10 (10½, 10½, 11) inches. *Shape armholes:* At beginning of each of the next 2 rows bind off 5 (5, 5, 6) stitches. Dec 1 stitch each end of needle every other row 3 (3, 4, 3) times. Work even until armholes measure 7¼ (7½, 7¾), 8) inches. *Shape Shoulders:* At beginning of each of next 4 rows bind off 6 (6, 7, 7) stitches. At the beginning of the next 2 rows, bind off 6 stitches twice. Bind off remaining stitches.

Left Front: Using smaller needles, cast on 34 (36, 38, 40) stitches. Knit 2, purl 2 in ribbing for 3¼ inches. Change to larger needles and work in stockinette. In first row, increase 1 stitch in first stitch and spread 3 more increases evenly along the row. Work evenly in stockinette until the piece measures 10 (10½, 10½, 11) inches. *Shape armhole and neck:* At the arm edge, bind off 5 (5, 5, 6) stitches, work to last 3 stitches, sl 1, knit 1, psso, Knit 1 (1 decrease at neck edge). Decrease 1 stitch at arm edge every other row 3 (3, 4, 3) times and *at the same time* decrease 1 stitch at neck edge every 4th row 5 (6, 6, 7) times more. Work even until armhole measures 7¼ (7½, 7¾, 8) inches. *Shape shoulder:* At the arm edge bind off 8 (9, 10, 11) stitches once and 8 stitches twice.

Right Front: Work to correspond with left front, reversing all shaping.

Sleeves: Using smaller needles cast on 48 (50, 52, 54) stitches. Knit 2, purl 2 for 2½ inches. Change to larger needles and stockinette. Increase 1 stitch in first stitch and increase 3 more stitches spread evenly across row. Continue to work in stockinette until piece measures 5 inches. *Shape cap:* At the beginning of each of the next 2 rows, bind off 5 (5, 5, 6) stitches. Decrease 1 stitch each end of needle every other row for 4½ (4¾, 5, 5¼) inches. At the beginning of each of the next 6 rows bind off 2 stitches. Bind off remaining stitches.

Finishing: Sew underarm, shoulder and sleeve seams. Set in sleeves. Single crochet 1 inch band around front and neck, spacing 5 button holes along right front. Sew buttons on left front. I use white mother-of-pearl buttons with white angora, dark mother-of-pearl with fawn, and fancy pewter buttons with gray.

WEAVING WITH ANGORA

Once upon a time, all clothing was laboriously made by hand, and in some parts of the world, it still is. In our industrial society ready-made clothing is available and inexpensive. Handweaving has become an art form—it speaks of love, devotion, and time. From this perspective it only makes sense to use fine luxury fibers like angora for handweaving.

I bought my first loom from weaver Joyce Scott, who gave me my introductory lessons. I think she felt guilty about selling her 8-shaft loom to someone who didn't even know what the shafts were for. Her most compelling advice concerned, not the mechanics of weaving, but the philosophy of fiber art. She told me that the most common mistake weavers made was trying to cut corners in the amount of yarn used in each project. "Never be stingy with fiber," she told me. "It's the substance of your project."

Pure handspun angora is surely the epitome of luxury in handweaving. Many weavers I've spoken to will hardly consider *any* handspun warp, much less an angora one. But the warp is fully half of the fiber content of most wearables. It is the foundation of the fabric. Warp yarn is never "wasted". The dimensions and concept of the fabric are woven into it. You should value your time and your weaving skills enough to invest in the right materials—and that includes a handspun angora warp.

Handweavers have two advantages over knitters when designing and working with pure angora. First, handweavers are likely to have more experience with relatively inelastic fibers such as cotton and silk, whereas knitters most often work with springy wool. Weavers are not as committed to working from patterns as knitters. It is quite likely that you can bring to mind projects you have woven which can be adapted to angora. Doubleweave sweaters, overshirts, shawls, co-coons (shawls with sleeves—add knit cuffs), vests, and tabards are wonderful woven in pure angora.

The same characteristics that knitters must consider when working with angora apply to weavers as well. Handwoven garments are often loose fitting, with wide necks and sleeves. These styles are ideal for keeping angora comfortable. Beware of knitted-on collars and cuffs. They not only trap heat, but can stretch out of shape.

Angora yarn itself is so richly textured that simple lines and patterns are the most logical choices. Plain weave and twills are the best weave structures for pure angora fabrics. Complicated patterns will become totally lost. The twill is used not so much for pattern as it is for structure. It adds body, accentuates texture, and helps maintain garment shape. Use floating selvedges when weaving twill fabric. Plain weave has less body than twill, but can still be used, especially if the yarn is fairly slubby. Use a light weight yarn and an open sett. Both twills and plain weave should be woven with the same number of weft picks as warp ends per inch, with a gentle press rather than a strong beat.

Handspun angora in no way resembles the lightly spun, short-staple angora in most commercial yarns. Any weaver would hesitate to subject such a fragile yarn to the abrasions of weaving. Long-staple angora spun with plenty of twist and plied makes excellent warp yarn. I have used both of my standard two-ply yarns for warp: the heavier (55 yd/oz) at 4 or 5 e.p.i. and the finer (110 yd/oz) at 5 or 7 e.p.i. I prefer the finer because the heavier is too heavy for most woven wearables. Both are difficult to break when tugged on, and therefore pass the most rigorous strength test for warp yarns. Take note that yarns too weak to pass this test can also be used as warp, because the tension in the warp is spread over the united strength of all the warp ends. Pure angora singles are strong enough, but fray apart from the friction of heddles and reed. Warp yarns should be spun and plied on large bobbins in order to minimize waste caused by many leftover ends shorter than warp length. You can economize on angora warp by tying onto a dummy warp left on the back beam.

Handspun angora does not require warp sizing, because it is smooth when it is spun. There are several tricks of the trade to using handspun warp that reduce the risk of fraying. Double sleying in a reed of wider sett reduces friction. Raising just one shed at a time decreases the amount of wear and tear when creating a shed. Wrapping the loom back-to-front avoids dragging the entire length of the warp through the reed and heddle. Use maximum tension when you tie on and while you weave with an angora warp, but be sure to relax the warp when you're not weaving.

Even if you can't be persuaded to try an angora warp, you can make lovely projects with a wool warp and an angora weft. However, an angora weft woven on a wool warp is nothing like pure angora. A fabric of wool and angora has a heavier hand, is stronger and more durable, and has wider variations in texture. The angora fluff is tied down, literally, by the wool warp. The effect is similar to a sweater knit from a single ply of angora and a single ply of wool. The two fibers maintain a lot of their own integrity. The finer the yarns and the tighter the weave structure, the more homogeneous the fabric appears.

The angora weft can be two-ply or single. A two-ply yarn is stronger and tends to better maintain garment shape. A single-ply yarn, on the other hand, is strong enough for weft and can usually be blocked to shape. Because it takes less than half the time to spin the same yardage in single as in two-ply yarn, single-ply is often the yarn of choice for weft.

I have used a single-ply angora yarn at 100 yd/oz as weft in many projects with a wool warp. The wool is textured enough to hold the slippery angora in a fairly loose weave so that the fabric is light and drapey. Silk is too slippery to hold angora securely in a loose weave. A project with a silk warp and angora weft would have to be planned carefully to create a weave tight enough to hold the yarns in place, but flexible enough for good hand and drape. I like to use a commercial 12/3s wool warp set at 6 e.p.i. with my singles angora weft. The fabric drapes beautifully and has an excellent hand. Shrinkage is about 10%. It is well suited to scarves, shawls and woven sweaters.

One of my favorite projects was a loose woven jacket with a striped wool warp and rainbow-dyed angora weft. First I dyed about 8 or 10 ounces of grade 1 angora in blues, purples and pinks, then spun the colorful fibers at 100 yards per ounce. I am indebted to Cindy Madden, an upstate New York weaver, for help designing the warp. I wanted to use a dark purple yarn (commercial 12/3s wool), but didn't have enough for such a large project. Cindy had some of the same yarn in lavender. By alternating one lavender warp with two dark purple ones, I had enough yarn to make my jacket. The two-toned warp enhanced the colorful rainbow dyes and broke up some of the stripiness. My "problem" had turned into a lucky design opportunity.

A favorite handwoven project was suggested by Cindy. I love to see (and feel!) angora yarn randomly interspersed in the warp of a silk or fine wool fabric. For shawls and scarves, this has the added benefit of putting the angora in the fringe. A mixed warp can be tricky and even frustrating, but it is definitely worth the effort. The trick to weaving on a mixed warp is to avoid messing with it, even if it looks like the angora is at a different tension than all the other yarns. When winding on the warp, do not alter the tension of the angora warp threads. During weaving, you will probably find it almost impossible to resist pulling and adjusting the angora warp ends, which will sag out from the shed. Ignore them. Pulling at them can distort the fabric. Without attention they will weave in just fine. I wish I could provide for each of you a sample of the fabric for my Silk Symphony shawl, so you could experience its softness.

"Silk Symphony" combines the softness of angora with shimmering silk. About a fourth of the warp ends are handspun angora for a fluffy fringe. Remaining warp and weft are 12/2 silk. Instructions follow.

SILK SYMPHONY SHAWL

Fabric description: Plain weave. Handspun angora is randomly interspersed in the primarily silk warp.

Size: 24 inches by 84 inches, plus fringe.

Warp: Handspun angora yarn, 2-ply, 110 yds/oz, 2.5 ounces (spin a little extra). 12/2s Super White Cultivated Silk, 3000 yds/lb (from Halcyon Yarns), 12 ounces (buy a pound).

Weft: Same silk yarn as above. Amount included above.

E.P.I.: 12

Warp Length: 3½ yds. Allows 35 inches loom waste (part used for fringe).

Width in Reed: 26 inches

Total Warp Ends: 312 (237 silk, 75 angora, randomly interspersed).

Weave: Plain weave, balanced with silk until piece is 94 inches long. Hemstitch edges on loom. Cut off, leaving enough warp for knots and fringe. Knot fringe in groups of six. Wash gently in a small amount of hot water with lots of a neutral detergent such as Joy. Squeeze and press, but do not agitate, twist, or wring. Rinse, dry and fluff up according to the directions starting on page 92.

Whatever your project, you must first make a sample. Handspun angora is so expensive, you cannot afford to have a project come out less than perfect. The yarn you "waste" on samples will be so much less than the yarn truly wasted in disappointing projects. Besides, samples (and notes) can be kept for future reference or to display to customers or at programs. I like to weave a sample 8 inches wide and 2 yards long. You should measure your sample on the loom, off the loom, and after it has been washed, finished, and dried. This will give you a complete understanding of how the fabric looks, feels, and behaves. Shrinkage for angora is usually around 10%. You should make a sample for each new handspun project, even if you have directions like the ones in this chapter. Variations in handspun yarn are almost unavoidable, and each weaver warps and weaves differently.

FURRY FANCIES

For a very pleasant span of time, on the last Saturday of each month, my life became more exciting, took on new perspectives. This was the day that I traveled an hour by car to meet with other spinners at our Saturday group guild meeting. Each month there were new ideas, new colors, new techniques, new fibers—all begging for attention. I fairly flew home after those meetings, renewed, invigorated, and eager to try a thousand new things. There is no way that I can replace for you the excitement and stimulation of a good spinning guild. Instead, I offer you this potpourri of projects to spark your imagination.

Outerwear accessories make wonderful small angora projects. I usually use my heavier two-ply yarn (55 yd/oz) for hats and mittens. A light weight yarn such as my 110 yd/oz two-ply is more appropriate for scarves, cowls, gloves, and baby clothing. Use your favorite pattern for machine or handknitting. Be sure to start with a gauge sample.

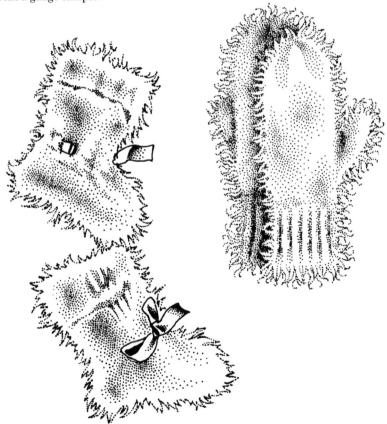

Hats make ideal angora projects. Elegant, stylish, and conspicuous, they focus a lot of attention on the angora. Styles with simple lines and plain stitches best set off angora's texture. With normal use, the delicate fibers are not subject to undue abrasion.

Berets are stylish in 100% angora and are easy to handknit. Make sure the headband portion is tight, because angora doesn't have a lot of elasticity. Alternately, knit a casing and insert elastic. You can knit a beret on a knitting machine, but you will have to knit it in pie-shaped segments along the radius of the beret, using short row technique. Use a dinner plate to block the finished beret.

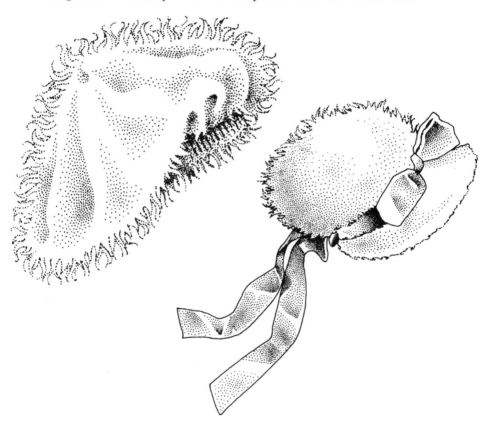

For machine knitters, I have a hat pattern that is extremely quick and easy. It takes about 1½ ounces of heavy two-ply yarn and only 20 minutes to knit. The simple lines are made elegant by the fluffiness of angora. It is so light that sometimes I have forgotten that I am wearing a hat, but it is incredibly warm even in cold upstate New York winters. (I even had a customer complain that it was too warm!)

PURE ANGORA HAT

Machine: Singer or Studio 360

Yarn: Handspun angora, 55 yds/oz

Gauge: 4 sts/in. 5 rows/in.

Tension: EON #8

Cast on 88 stitches. Knit in stockinette for 30 rows. Turn hem by putting stitches from first knit row onto needles. Knit in stockinette for 45 additional rows. Slip every other stitch onto its neighboring needle (decrease every other stitch). Knit 1 row. Break yarn so that you have a "tail" of about 20 inches. Thread yarn onto large sewing needle and pick up all remaining stitches. Draw tight and knot. Sew side seam.

Scarves, which coordinate so well with hats, are not as suitable for angora as one might think. Wrapping them around necks, knotting them, and tucking them into coats results in considerable abuse. Angora is such a good insulator that the neck it is wrapped around gets moist, increasing the risk of felting. Knit scarves tend to stretch and become thinner in areas which habitually encircle the neck. Woven scarves hold up better. You could handknit a delicate scarf worn primarily as a decorative accent.

Most knitting machines will not knit a double faced fabric suitable for angora scarves. You must either knit (in a fine angora yarn) a fabric twice as wide as you want the scarf to be and double it over with a side seam, or knit in a rib stitch which has rather the same doubling effect. In either case, you end up using twice the amount of yarn necessary for a scarf, which is an appalling waste of angora, especially because even a single layer of angora is so warm to start with. In any case, scarves are not always "little" projects. A long, dramatic winter scarf may take nearly as much yarn as a sweater.

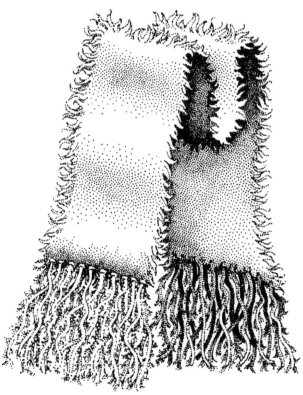

A good alternative to a scarf is a cowl. This attractive accessory consists of a knitted cylinder which drapes gracefully around the neckline, but is long enough to be pulled up over the head as well. A cowl can be woven seamlessly with double-weave, or handknit in the round in a fine two-ply yarn of 100% angora. This style avoids the wrapping, knotting, and tucking of scarves while still being attractive and functional.

A young man once bought a pair of pure angora mittens from me. It was the Christmas season and they were to be a present for his grandmother. "Grandmother," he told me, "can't hear or see very well anymore, but she can still *feel*." There was so much love and caring in his eyes that I could just picture the old woman caressing the softness of the mittens on her hands and smiling.

For the most part, mittens of pure angora are not suited for daily wear by active people. But the tighter they are knit the more durable they are, and they are certainly a treat to wear on special occasions. I once had a pair of pure angora gloves, tightly knit of the finest yarn spun from gray English angora. I was so enamored of them and they were so warm, I wore them continually and they lasted a whole winter's season. What really did them in was the weight and pressure of the heavy satchel I carried in my right hand. This shrank the inside of the right mitten so that it became permanently shaped in the form of a clasping hand. Pure angora mittens are worth considering if you suffer from very cold hands. The instant warmth is amazing and the softness never irritates cold, chapped hands. For extra durability you could use a blend with wool.

I also make angora-blend legwarmers. Pure angora is too warm for indoor legwarmers and so fluffy that it abrades with free leg movement. I use a single ply of angora and a single ply of Merino wool and this seems to form a good balance between warmth, softness, and functionality. Legwarmers are so easy to knit, being merely a long tube with ribbing on each end. Like scarves, legwarmers are not exactly "little" projects and, in fact, take quite a bit of yarn.

Although soft and warm, angora will shrink and felt if worn when wet. So remember to remove any damp or snowy angora accessories as soon as possible and allow them to air dry.

A Touch of Angora

A little bit of pure angora trim is an inexpensive way to jazz up a plain sweater or blouse. An angora collar alone or with matching cuffs adds pizazz to a classic garment. The accessory can be small and plain, relying exclusively on the texture and softness of the angora for effect, or it may be as fancy as you like. Lace is so romantic and feminine. In fine white angora the pattern will be subtle but evident. Collars make good projects for angora lace, as they suffer no abuse from friction or body moisture. Mounting an angora collar on a dickey allows it to be easily removed for wardrobe versatility and cleaning. Cuffs, being close to the hands, are more likely to be subject to abrasion.

You can incorporate a little bit of angora for accent into your larger knitwear or handweaving projects. Accents can range from simple vertical or horizontal stripes woven in angora to complex patterns and designs. I saw a handwoven jacket on display in a small Adirondack museum. Unfortunately, I do not remember the name of the weaver, but she was from upstate New York. The jacket was woven in several colors of natural wool and was accented with two narrow panels of angora bordering the front opening. The use of angora here was subtle and effective.

The jacket used angora in a plain weave, but you can also use angora in pattern weaving. Many years ago I wove a hooded scarf of wool and angora with rosepath trim in pure white angora. A hooded scarf is one woven wide enough so that a hood is formed when the scarf is folded in half and stitched together on one side for about 12 inches from the fold. Avoid using just one broad band of pattern. Introduce the eye to the pattern by weaving in narrow related bands on either side with narrow margins in between.

Knitted angora edgings are wonderful. Just a few rows of angora around the collar or bodice can really set off a sweater. As little as an ounce of angora can produce a dramatic effect. Four ounces of heavy two-ply angora used as pattern yarn will put a frosty trim on an Icelandic-style sweater. The complex patterns are softened by the fluffy texture. You might think that all that angora carried across the inside of the sweater would be wasted—until you feel it against your skin.

You can also use angora in more modern designs. Stripes can be vertical or horizontal, symmetrical or asymmetrical. Chevrons can run down the body or the arms. Trim sleeve edges or make entire sleeves from angora contrasting with a wool or silk bodice of another color. Run angora cables up the front or down the sleeves. Try some dyed angora in a Kaffe Fassett-style pattern. Trim the tops of socks.

One of my favorite sweaters is a machine-knit one that I named "Sandstorm" (photo page 74). It has vertical stripes of angora, alpaca, and two kinds of handspun silk (which had won first prize in the New York State Fair). It is accented with pure angora sleeves and an antique lace collar. The sleeves are finished with hand-crocheted angora and the bottom ribbing is alpaca. All the fibers are natural colors.

Erika Baker's sweater, "Winter Scenery," is stunning with artistically placed sections of my handspun angora, as well as cotton, alpaca, silk, and wool. Erika says that there are at least 40 different shades of yarn. The body was knit on a Brother 230 knitting machine, and the trim at the neckline, wrists and waist is hand finished. "Mountains" is another Erika Baker creation, machine-knit in one piece from the bottom up in wool, silk, alpaca, and my own handspun angora yarn.

Angora has some specialty uses as well. It is perfectly suited for animal motifs on sweaters, especially bunnies and kittens. These can be knit or woven in or embroidered on later. Needleworkers can also use angora to add life-like texture to furry creatures in their embroidery projects. Clouds and snow are well represented by angora in scenic designs. Let your imagination fly.

You might have some very lumpy or heavily spun angora yarn from beginning spinning or from spinning lower grade angora. Don't throw it out. You can use it for texture in weaving projects such as wall hangings or pillows. Or take a wool knitting yarn of about the same diameter as your heavy angora yarn and knit them together (as if one yarn) into super-warm hats and mittens.

Odds and Ends

In a less aristocratic form, angora can be used in many novelty items. One of my favorites is knitted or crocheted bunnies done in handspun angora. You can find patterns for these at many knit shops. To get the furriest effect, use a tight gauge. I heard of a woman who sold very tiny furry animals made from angora, using colored angora for little puppy dogs and bears and white for rabbits. Clearly these could not have been toys for small children. I imagine them to be more akin to the pipe cleaner and fleece "sheep" sold at craft fairs.

Fluffy angora was made to order for the winter holiday season. Most likely you can find more places to use angora in Christmas ornaments and decorations than I have thought of—snow, Santa's beard, and angel hair. Rabbit raisers, here is one place where you actually can use some of those matts, especially the kind which are matted at the base of the fiber, but with tips flowing free like velvet.

My favorite Christmas project for angora is a wide band of white trim around the top of Christmas stockings sewn from old quilts. These have an old fashioned charm and make delightful gifts when stuffed with homemade sweets.

Felting Angora

The Mad Hatter at the famous tea party with Alice and the dormouse wasn't always insane. We now know that the mercury used in hat manufacturing was poisonous and that years of exposure would render an individual quite literally mad. The mercury was used in a process called carroting to expand and open the microscopic scales of rabbit fur so that it would felt more securely. People who know this bit of lore often assume that angora rabbit hair doesn't felt on its own. Anyone who has combed a matted rabbit or machine washed and dried an angora sweater knows differently.

Felt fabric is made by shrinking and pounding cloth or fibers to give a smooth, tight finish. Folklore attributes the discovery of felt to St. Clement, the patron saint of hatters, who put some loose wool in his shoes for comfort during a long walk. Angora felts just like wool. Moisture, heat, detergent, and agitation force the fibers into closer and closer contact, forming the dense mat of fabric we know as felt. Normally you try to avoid this phenomenon. Here, I do an about face and tell you the virtues of angora felt.

In felt, angora retains its characteristic softness and warmth, but it does not fluff up or become textured like angora yarn. In fact, it is smoother than wool felt because the fibers themselves are finer and smoother and can compact more tightly. I've used angora felt for hats and to make liners for sheepskin slippers after the fleecy bottoms have worn thin.

Angora added to a wool felt project will add softness and lightweight warmth. You can blend the angora thoroughly, create texture by blending in nubs and slubs of angora, or put a top layer of pure angora over your wool felt. Do keep in mind that angora does not have the water repellent properties of wool.

You can use any procedure for felting angora that you would use for wool. I use grade 2 angora for making pure angora felt, and grade 3 for adding texture to wool angora blends. In all cases you start with carded batts.

Pure angora usually has to be carded on hand cards or on a small drum carder, which puts some limits on project size. The cottage carding machines which make large batts are ideal for making angora-blend felts, and the large size allow one to contemplate some major felting projects. After aligning the carded fibers in alternating layers (fibers of different layers should run perpendicular to each other) and sewing them into nylon screens, pillow cases or such, you can stomp on them in buckets of hot soapy water or throw them in the washer and dryer, and otherwise proceed with your usual felting routine. There are many fine books on felting if you need more specific directions.

TO LAST A LIFETIME

Noted silkworker Jean Case often begins her programs by displaying a natty tussah silk jacket which she says is ten years old and has been washed dozens of times. It amazes those of us who see silk as a delicate luxury fiber, not suited for daily wear. She also dazzles us by passing around dozens of silk garments and flourishing great expanses of expensive fiber as she demonstrates dyeing, reeling, or spinning. I've been amazed at how casually she handles hundreds, maybe thousands of dollars worth of silk.

Many years later, I now realize that other spinners see me and my angora in the same light. Angora is not as delicate as the princess of pea renown. I think you'll be surprised at how durable long staple, handspun angora is. By minding a few common-sense rules, angora will last a life time.

Angora is dry cleanable, but dry cleaning has several disadvantages. It is expensive and dry cleaners do not reimburse you for the value of your handmade angora sweater should it be damaged. Many people don't realize that handspun angora can be washed by hand. It grows fluffier and more beautiful with each washing.

The guidelines for hand washing angora are much the same as for wool. Angora garments are not usually as bulky as wool, so handling is actually easier. "Hand wash warm water. Lay flat to dry." So says the label, but this doesn't really tell you a lot. Here are my washing instructions.

Fill a sink or basin with lukewarm water. The water should feel neither warm nor cool to your hand. For the very first washing, I use slightly warmer water and a small amount of Joy detergent to clean out the oil. Angora doesn't have but about 1% by weight of oil in its fleece, but getting it out does make it softer. For subsequent washes, you can use one of those cleaners especially made for "fine washables". Swish the detergent around to distribute it throughout the water and then add the angora sweater. Angora is difficult to wet thoroughly, so squeeze the sweater gently but firmly while holding it under water to remove all the air bubbles. Repeat this procedure several times. It may help to let the sweater soak for 15 or 20 minutes. Squeezing also forces the water through and past individual fibers so that the dirt is washed away. When you are through with the washing, carefully pour off the wash water (or pull the plug and let the water run out of the sink) and (again, gently!) squeeze out excess water from the sweater.

Do not lift up a soaking wet angora sweater. The weight of the water—which is considerable—will pull and stretch the fibers. Angora doesn't have a lot of elasticity to begin with and this kind of wet stretching will not help it any. Squeeze excess water out of the sweater and lift it with full support, cradling it in both hands. Rinse it twice in clean, fresh, lukewarm water, squeezing to move water past the fibers as in the washing process. After the final rinse, squeeze the sweater (do not wring or twist) dry as possible.

The next step—the old fashioned method to further remove excess water—would be to lay the sweater on a towel, wrap the towel around the sweater, and roll it up. This transfers much of the water from the sweater to the towel. The towel can more easily be dried in the drier (although it will pick up some angora fluff). However, this is the point where I diverge from standard methods of caring for fine washables.

For ten years I lived on a homestead farm and washed my laundry in a wringer washer and hung it on a line to dry, summer and winter. Although I still prefer country life to the city (I spend my summers at a mountain camp with no phone, no electricity and no running water, except the brook), the inventions I cherish the most are modern laundry equipment, both for private use and especially for my business.

The spin cycle on my washing machine removes more excess water from washed angora sweaters than any number of towels. The centrifugal force of the spinning presses the water out without twisting or stretching the fibers. **You cannot use your washing machine to wash angora sweaters.** Use the *spin cycle only* to press out excess water. First, squeeze out as much water as you can with your hands and place the sweater carefully into the empty washing machine, arranging it so that it is neither bunched up nor stretched out. You will need some other object to balance the machine, either another freshly washed sweater or a large towel. (One of the joys of this system, especially if you are into production, is that you can easily do several at a time.) Shut the lid of the washer and turn the control knob past any wash or rinse cycles to "spin" and turn on the machine. Remove the sweater from the machine immediately after spinning dry. It only takes a couple of minutes.

I find large nylon mesh sweater drying racks invaluable for drying angora sweaters. Mine have little plastic feet so I can set them up anywhere that is convenient—outside in summer shade, inside over a heat register or out of the way in the guest bedroom. They also come equipped with cords so that they can be hung from the ceiling. There are the kinds that rest on the bath tub as well. If you do not have a sweater dryer, you can make do with a table or other large flat surface covered with towels. You will have to turn the sweater over several times and change the towels as they absorb water from it, which is a bother. This process may ruin the finish of a wooden table. Use an extra layer of newspaper under the towels if you must use wood.

Angora has some memory and tends to hold the shape it dries in. Take care as you lay out your sweater to dry that all the seam lines are straight and that the sleeves and collar are aligned properly. Don't forget to check that the back (which you can't see) is symmetrical with the front. Angora doesn't have as much elasticity as wool, and stretches even more when wet. Ease the ribbing into its most compact structure in order to preserve as much elasticity as possible and also to take advantage of the memory. The sweater will dry in one to two days, depending on its thickness and the temperature and humidity. Do not leave an angora sweater to dry in the sun, which will bleach out dye and even worse, damage the fibers. Avoid drying angora near any strong heat source, as well. I can get away with drying my sweaters over heat registers for two reasons. First, the legs of the sweater dryer hold the sweater away from direct heat and second, my house is only heated to about 64°F in winter.

Now it is time to use your electric dryer, not to dry your sweater (it is already dry), but to fluff it up. You can't comb or brush up the nap on angora like you can mohair or wool. The fibers are just too delicate. Angora will fluff up on its own accord in the course of time. Unfortunately, customers don't want to pay hundreds of dollars for a sweater which is not fluffy *right now*. So before I had a dryer, I spent hours developing ingenious ways of hastening the process. Placing the sweater outside on a breezy day will do it. The breeze from a window or a hair dryer set on "air" **(not heat)** will also work. These methods are, however, time consuming and fussy. Nothing works as well as a dryer set on air dry.

The dryer technique must be used with extreme care and caution. Place the *fully dry* angora sweater in the dryer. A dry towel or other sweater put in with it will increase the static electricity which brings up the fluff. Turn the dryer on to the *"air only"* cycle **(no heat)** and let it run for five minutes and **no longer.** Check the sweater. Most likely it has not fluffed up enough, so put it back in (on air only, no heat) for another five minutes only, and check again. It will usually take two to four five-minute cycles to fluff up your sweater. However, minute differences in fiber structure, fabric structure and relative humidity affect how quickly this happens. Too much tossing in the dryer, and you have felt. So you must check every five minutes or risk ruining your sweater. After several years of using this method successfully, I thought I had a good handle on exactly how much time was needed for a sweater to fluff up. I got tired of running downstairs to the dryer every five minutes and so set the timer for ten minutes at one point in the cycle and came back to find the sweater was no longer the same size or structure that it was before. And though I teased and tugged and prayed and swore, there was nothing to do except remake the $450 custom order during the Christmas rush.

A spinner usually doesn't want to fluff up angora yarns. They are easier to work with in their newly spun, smooth state, whether knitting or weaving. However, there are a few instances where you might want to display a fluffy yarn—a state fair entry for example. The easiest and most reasonable way to fluff up angora yarn is to spin it well in advance (as in weeks or even months) and let daily gentle breezes tease out the ends into delightful fluff. Many of us are not so organized and well prepared as to plan so far ahead. I know one woman who finished spinning and dyeing her angora yarn the night before entries were due for the New York State Fair. The yarn was still damp in the morning, so she tied the skein to the antenna of her car and drove to the fair. By the time she arrived the skein was dry and fluffy. If it became overly tangled, she never told me. I can't remember if it won a prize.

You can also fluff up yarn in the dryer, but this is even more tricky than fluffing up a sweater. Tie the skein in 16 places for a two-yard skein, more tightly than for dyeing. Toss the *dry* skein in the dryer on air (no heat) at five minute intervals just as for a sweater. In five to 15 minutes you will have all the fluff you need. However, many of the ends of the fluff will be attached one to the other, so that the strands of yarn are somewhat united. To remedy this, place the skein on a skein winder, rewind it into a ball, and then reskein it. Clearly this is a lot of extra trouble, but it works in a pinch. Be very careful to stop the fluffing before the yarns become irrevocably tangled.

If you ever want to fluff up a woven garment which has an angora fringe, you can still use the dryer. Tie the fringe threads in groups of five with coated wire quick-ties. After tossing, remove the ties and comb through the fringe with your fingers (it will be tangled).

Storing Angora

If you visit my studio, you will find my angora sweaters gently nestled in tissue-lined gift boxes. I do this for the sake of the customers (and sales) who believe that angora must be treated like a delicate princess. In reality, angora takes much more abuse than you can imagine. Three angora sweaters, rolled up into a carrying case, rode in the back of my truck all summer long, waiting to be shown to a bartering customer who never appeared. I try to keep the sweaters in my cedar chest neatly folded, but in the eternal rush of life, it seems that everything becomes as jumbled as a child's sock drawer. When it comes to storing angora garments, there are only three important factors to remember. You must protect your angora from moths, humidity, and compression.

Compression can occur either from flattening the sweater down with heavy objects or from squeezing it into too small a space. Compression takes the life out of angora, squeezing out what little elasticity it does have. Give your angora garment plenty of room to relax and stretch out. Even under the best of circumstances, an angora garment which has been in storage for several months will seem a little flat. You can bring it back to life with a quick five-minute toss in the dryer on *air only* (**no heat**).

Humidity is any kind of moisture or dampness. It is relatively easy to avoid. It means not storing your angora in a damp basement or in the same drawer as a sweaty jogging suit. Within the living areas of a normal house in a temperate zone, humidity is not usually a problem.

Wool moths, however, often are. Moths like angora much better than wool. Angora is the créme de la créme of the wool moth diet. I once stored (for too long a time) a lavender blend of angora and wool. The moth larvae ate the angora all the way through the several pounds of carded fiber and never touched the wool.

I want to go into a little more detail about moths, because it is one of the few topics pertaining to wool which is not adequately covered in most textile publications. Either it's a taboo subject or we're all supposed to know about it already. However, anyone can have trouble with moths. Eggs can come in on fiber you purchase, imported wall hangings, and woolen pillows. As for myself, I grew up in a polyester household. My mother had five children and was thoroughly devoted to wash and wear. So I didn't even recognize the first wool moth larvae I saw. I took them to my vet, because they were moving around in some angora fiber I'd plucked off a rabbit purchased just the day before. I thought maybe they were a parasite or something.

The descendants from a single pair of wool moths can eat about 50 pounds of wool in one year. It is the larvae of the wool moths, tiny little worm-like critters, that do the eating. They eat not only angora or wool sweaters, but animal fibers of all sorts—wool carpets, wall hangings, cushions, fur coats, wool-blend clothing, and even feathers. They can subsist on dry milk, dried skin, dead insects, and the lint embedded in floor boards. They do not eat plant fibers. They rarely eat silk.

There are a couple of different species. The main difference that you would notice is that one type carries around with it a little cylindrical cocoon-like sac which it hides in, and the other crawls around naked. The most important one is the webbing clothes moth, *Tineola bisselliella*. Its larvae spin silky webs as they feed, which are left in a mass over the cloth. The case-making clothes moth, *Tinea pellionella*, is similar to its cousin, except that it spins silken threads, which it blends with the fabric it eats, to make a case which it lives in and carries on its back. It can withdraw into the case, so you can't see the larva at all, or it can crawl around, nearly fully extended, dragging its case like a snail with a shell. Both eat constantly.

Adult wool moths have a wing span of about 1/2 inch. They do not eat at all. They are not attracted to light as are most moths. Their primary concern is reproduction.

Tiny and tan, you may have seen them flitting around a room. If I remember correctly from my farm days, they tend to come out in the evening. Their flight is erratic and you can chase them around and around without great success. When they land on a surface, they crawl in crazy patterns, but they can also make a rapid bee-line for any hiding place—under carpets, behind furniture, even under a piece of paper or fabric. It is amazing what a tiny space they can crawl into.

Killing airborne wool moths is entertaining and somewhat vindicating, but it won't help control their reproduction. The moths you can see are all males. All they do is fly around and look for the females, who are heavy with eggs and hiding in some invisible nook or cranny. If even one male escapes your vigilance, there will soon be a new army of larvae marching towards your fibers.

The female wool moth, while preferring wool or angora or fur for her eggs, is not compulsive about her preference. In the absence of an ideal substrate, she will lay her eggs in any suitable dark corner—even between floor boards. Each female lays 100 to 150 small white eggs, which are only 1/50 inch long. They hatch in a few days to several weeks depending on the temperature and humidity. When the larvae hatch out they are so tiny that they can crawl between individual cloth fibers. The larval stage can last from six weeks to four years (eating every chance they get). When the larvae are full grown (about 3/8 inch long), they spin a cocoon and three to six weeks later emerge as adult moths. So the entire life cycle of the wool moth can go as quickly as a few months to as long as several years.

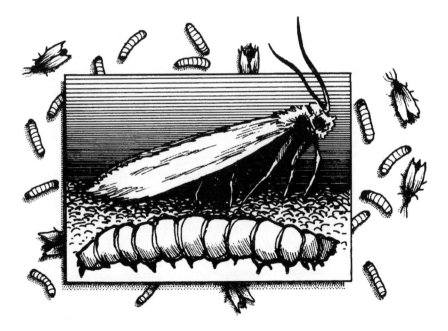

Wool moth larvae prefer angora to wool. Center shows magnified look at an adult wool moth (top) and a larva (bottom).

Such is the life cycle of the wool moth: adults, eggs, larvae, cocoons, adults. The amount of time it takes to complete this cycle depends primarily on the temperature. The warmer the temperature, the faster the cycle. The cycle stops temporarily at low temperatures. This is the reason that expensive furs are kept in cold storage for the summer (below 45°F). Freezing for extended periods, alternating cold and warm temperatures, dry cleaning, and sunning kill all stages.

Moth proofing treatments for fibers are too harsh for angora, so you must find other ways of protecting your angora from moths. Considering the extent of my inventory, I am rabid about moth protection. Herbal sachets and cedar repel moths, but I rely on and always use moth balls—the old fashioned naphthalene ones. They stink to high heaven, but they *kill* moths, eggs and larvae. The odor clings and the moth balls last a long time. The paradichlorobenzene variety has an odor which disperses more rapidly (of course, they don't last as long either) and you may prefer these. I like the confidence inspired by the strong smell of the naphthalene. In order to be really effective, moth balls and woolens must be kept tightly sealed.

Cedar contains repellent oils which deter, but do not kill, wool moths. A good cedar chest is an excellent place to store angora and other fine woolens. I supplement mine with moth balls as well. The lid of the cedar chest should have a lip on the inside as well as on the outside, to prevent moths from entering. They can crawl through the tiniest cracks.

Remember that all angora or wool garments must be absolutely clean before storing. Invisible moth eggs may lurk in an unwashed garment. While in storage, the eggs will hatch out and the larvae will eat holes in everything they can get their little pinchers onto. That may mean not only the sweater they rode in on, but every other garment in the cedar chest or drawer as well. No amount of cedar oil or herbs are going to stop them once they get in there. They have all summer to munch away. Clean before you store!

Good housekeeping is, in fact, one of the best wool moth deterrents. Frequent vacuuming of rugs (both sides) and wall hangings removes lint and hair, as well as any eggs which may have been laid there. Throw out those old fleeces and scraps of yarn and fabric you know you will never use. Don't forget about your sample books. Check them regularly or store them in moth balls.

Although I have had moths in raw fiber and occasionally in yarn, I have never had a sweater damaged. I protect my finished garments like a fiend. It would be fairly easy to repair your own sweater—angora's fur and fluff would hide most small mends. But to sell, my garments must be perfect and I have too much time invested in my inventory. I think you can imagine the content of my worst nightmares.

Producing Your Own Fiber

I BEGAN RAISING ANGORA RABBITS BECAUSE I WAS AT A STAGE IN MY LIFE DURING which it was important to me to see connections in the world. In a modern life which had made no sense to me, I was searching for satisfaction in creating something new and useful and even beautiful where nothing had been before.

My other motivation was more prosaic: economy. My parents used to joke that if you turned me loose in a store with no visible price tags, I would pick out the most expensive items. I certainly zeroed in on that luxurious silk and angora vest at the silk workshop. I knew that I could never afford to buy it, so I would have to make it myself. Happily, it turns out that raising angora rabbits is economical—and you will be assured of the best quality fiber. It's not quite as lucrative as spinning straw into gold, but as one friend's husband commented upon hearing the price of angora yarn, "That's the price of silver!"

THE PERFECT PET

Rabbits make loving pets. Almost any spinner who loves animals can experience the pleasure of keeping an angora rabbit and working with its silky, soft fur. Any country farm, suburban house, or even an apartment that permits pets can accommodate one of these quiet, congenial animals. I knew a Flamenco dancer whose pet angora lived in a wooden box on the back porch and came inside daily to clean the dust balls from behind the furniture. A German angora buck I know has his own deluxe penthouse apartment in a barn, complete with a sunning porch overlooking a beautiful Adirondack lake. Unheated garages, basements, and barns shelter angora rabbits who often come in to the house to play with other pets and children. I knew an angora rabbit and a Danish wolfhound that were best friends. You can have the softest, most beautiful animal friend in addition to producing your own luxurious spinning fiber. Unless frightened or hurt, angoras are gentle animals which rarely bite or scratch. They are easy to care for and require no regular veterinary care or shots.

A silky soft bunny begging for a new home can be temptation incarnate for a fiber-lover. Even when I owned more than a hundred angora rabbits, the opportunity to buy a new one was always hard to resist. Cuddling one of these cute bundles of fluff was guaranteed to seal the deal. Many spinners buy the first rabbit they see, just as I did. From my experiences with this first and other impulsive purchases, I have learned that buying an angora rabbit merits some research and consideration. It takes only a few minutes to buy a rabbit, but it is a decision which you will have to live with—and feed—for years. Giving some thought to factors such as breed, sex, age, and colors can help you choose the rabbit which is best for you. Locating a reputable breeder and quality stock is also worth the extra effort in terms of health and productivity. So hold off a little while, if you can, and use the information in this chapter to help you select and buy your perfect pet angora.

The Case for a Single Bunny

A single angora rabbit, especially a high-producing German, can produce enough fiber to keep the average spinner busy with a variety of projects. Spun fine, the annual harvest from one rabbit will provide a spinner with some 75 hours of spinning and at least that many more hours of knitting or weaving. Add more time if you like to dye your yarn or blend the angora with other fibers. The pure angora alone is enough to make at least two major projects—and many more are possible if you blend or use the angora as accents or trim. Though we all have grand plans for ambitious projects, the fact is that most of us have lots of other things to do beside spin, and one or two big projects is all we can manage to fit into our busy schedules.

One rabbit also gives the best fiber production, because one rabbit is easier to take care of than two or three—or a dozen. We're busy, remember? And it is all too easy to let the grooming go an extra week until suddenly the fleece is all matted. That's *really* no fun, to say nothing of wasting all that fine angora fiber. So, because it is so easy and fast to groom just one rabbit, you will do it more often, keep the rabbit matt-free, and actually get more fiber than if you kept several rabbits and let them get matted even once or twice. Also, the complications of more than one rabbit include: extra cages, extra space, opportunities for fighting and wool chewing, increased chances of disease and infection, and possible breeding. All these things will either increase costs, decrease fiber production, or both. The point here is to provide you, the spinner, with a luxury fiber in an enjoyable, satisfying, and economical manner. You can do this best if you limit yourself to one (or at most two or three) rabbits. One rabbit is quite happy to live alone, especially if you have the time to be affectionate and care for him.

What will it cost?

Raising your own angora will more than pay for itself. Here's a little review of the basic economics of raising an angora rabbit as a pet for your own fiber use. Actual prices may vary with the years, but my current prices will serve as an example. You can buy a junior pedigreed German angora rabbit for $125. A suitable cage to keep in your garage or basement will cost about $50 from a rabbit equipment supply company. Other equipment you will need, such as combs, scissors, feeder, and waterer, will cost about $40 altogether. Your initial investment therefore is $215. You can amortize this amount over a period of at least five years, so that your annual cost is $43 per year. (The rabbit and equipment may well last longer, but we'll use five years as a very reasonable example.) It will cost you about $25 for a hundred pounds of pelletized food and another $12 for two bales of hay, totalling $37 per year for food. A well-cared-for rabbit does not normally require any veterinary attention. Therefore, the annual expense of raising an angora rabbit is $80. This German angora will produce two to three pounds of prime plucked fiber per year. Using 2½ pounds for our example, with a retail of $7.50 *per ounce*, the value of the fiber produced is $300. Can you get that kind of return on your investment if you spent the same money on a sheep?

Of course there are other factors is this computation. It doesn't take into account your time, or expenses such as advertising and overhead, which would be necessary if you were in the business of selling the fiber. However, that is the beauty of having a single angora pet. Yours is *not* a business. You don't have to advertize, rent space, etc., because *you* yourself are using the fiber. Keeping an angora rabbit is an enjoyable, economical way to produce your own high-quality spinning fibers.

After ten years of living on a homestead farm and raising every kind of farm animal, I am convinced that the least important factor in buying an animal is the initial purchase price, which ranges from free to over a hundred dollars. With rare exceptions, you get what you pay for and it costs the same amount in time and money to feed, house, and care for a poor animal as it does for a superior one. Usually the cheaper animal will be sick more often and incur more vet fees as well. It is extremely tempting to reach out for that "bargain", but if you spread out the initial purchase price over the lifetime of the rabbit, your "bargain" works out to little annual savings. A good-quality rabbit will not only be more productive, but will look better and be more satisfying to raise.

Sex, Age, and Color

Our current culture tends to view little girls as cute and charming and so many people assume that a female rabbit will make the better pet. Surprisingly, it is the male rabbit which is usually more personable. Bucks tend to be friendly, outgoing, and curious; I recommend them as pets because of their more interesting person- alities. Does, on the other hand, have a tendency to be more reserved, cautious, or even aggressive because (biologically speaking) they have the heavy responsi- bility of raising the next generation. These are just useful generalizations that can help you choose your rabbit. Individual variations—the friendly doe or the reserved buck—can occur, of course. Bucks are often more easily obtainable and sometimes are less expensive, because of the high demand for does by breeders. According to some studies, bucks seem to produce slightly less fiber overall than does. This difference is important if you multiply it over the hundreds of rabbits found in a commercial herd, but is hardly significant if you have only one animal.

The majority of angora rabbits are sold as "juniors" anywhere from weaning to just before maturity. Six to eight weeks is perhaps the most common age. Although it is possible to wean baby bunnies earlier than six weeks, it is generally not considered good breeding practice in this country. Young bunnies adapt readily and become affectionate pets. Unfortunately, it is difficult to evaluate the quality of the fleece so early, and baby fleece is not suitable for spinning. You will have to wait until your bunny is nine to 12 months old before harvesting mature fiber.

"Seniors" are rabbits of mature weight and age, usually about one year old or older. Breeders are often reluctant to sell seniors because even a much greater price doesn't usually adequately compensate for the investment in time, cage space, and feed. An adult angora is well worth a higher price because you can easily see and evaluate the fleece and personality. A mature rabbit, on the other hand, does not adapt as easily to a new home and new owner, especially as a pet. An older junior, say three months old, may be a suitable compromise between maturity and adaptability.

If you are going to have just one rabbit, white angora has the greatest design potential. You can use it unadorned in its classic elegance, dye it a rainbow of beautiful colors, or blend it with black wool for a soft gray yarn. On the whole, albino rabbits tend to produce more fiber than colored ones. (Blue-eyed whites and "Himalayans" are not albinos, and their fiber production may be somewhat lower on the average.) Natural colored angora blends nicely with naturally colored wool, and it can be dyed (see page 59). The more common colored angoras—fawn and black—may cost less than the exotic colored ones as well as be better fiber producers.

Breed

Although German angoras are far and away the best fiber producers, consider other factors when selecting a breed. You may prefer a color not available in the German lines. The furnishings (ear fringes, etc.) of the German and the English are cute, but they also take a lot of extra work to keep matt-free and don't provide you with spinnable fiber. The French angoras pluck quickly and easily, making that task a breeze. You may prefer the downy fineness of the English to the furriness of the French or German. Perhaps the tiny English are easier for you or your children to handle. Remember that no breed is "best"; learn the characteristics and choose the breed which suits you.

For example, say you're a spinner who has time for just one project per year (so you don't need the highest fiber producer); you prefer the natural fawn color because it goes with your own natural coloring (fawns aren't available in German angoras at this writing); you're a busy working mother, so you don't have much time for grooming and plucking (French are the easiest to care for); and you definitely like luscious furry angora. In this case, clearly a fawn French angora is the rabbit for you.

FINDING A RABBIT

Buy locally if at all possible, so that you can inspect the rabbits and see the condition of the rabbitry. Also, the breeder is *obligated by the sale* to give you help and advice in your new venture. (It is not reasonable to ask a local breeder to help or advise you on stock you bought elsewhere, unless you are going to pay a consulting fee.)

It you don't already know one, finding an angora breeder may be your most difficult task. The first place to check for breeders is your own spinning guild. Guild newsletters may have ads, and membership lists often include spinners' interests and fiber sources. You can check the county fair or 4-H clubs for angora rabbit raisers. These breeders will probably be emphasizing show rabbits rather than fiber producers, but these characteristics are not necessarily mutually exclusive.

If you have exhausted local possibilities, check for ads in national rabbit or fiber arts magazines. The National Angora Rabbit Breeders Club has a long list of angora breeders around the country. Write or call several breeders. When writing for information it is considerate to include a self-addressed stamped envelope.

Evaluating a Breeder

When asking about angora rabbits for sale, you may also make reasonable polite inquiries about the breeder. How long has the breeder been raising angoras? Does the breeder spin or sell angora to handspinners? Such a breeder may understand your needs better than one who concentrates on show animals, and be able to help you choose a good fiber producer. The breeder should be a member of the ARBA or the NARBC, or subscribe to their policies, which include a 30-day guarantee of health.

As a novice angora raiser, you may not find it easy to evaluate a rabbit breeder or his rabbits. Assessment skills improve with experience, which you don't yet have. However, you do have good judgment and common sense and I recommend that you use them in conjunction with the guidelines provided in this book. Do take all these cautions with a grain of salt. Assume that most breeders are reliable, know what they are doing, and have good stock to sell you. Just keep an eye out for obvious signs to the contrary.

If you can visit the rabbitry, you can get a good idea if the breeder is competent by making a few simple observations. A good rabbitry is clean, well-lit, and especially well-ventilated. Listen to the rabbits. You should not hear any sneezing. Regard with healthy skepticism any statements the breeder makes about the sneezing being caused by sawdust or dusty hay. Sometimes this is true, but maybe it isn't. Respiratory ailments can be quite troublesome in rabbits. Look over all the rabbits, not just the ones for sale. They should be well groomed and free of matts. They may not all be in full coat (in fact, most of them probably won't be), but there should not be any matted fleeces. The rabbits should not be crowded together in cages (except for mothers with their babies). A breeder who takes good care of his rabbits probably also takes pride in having good stock.

Checking a Rabbit's Health

You should be able to trust your breeder, but you also want to have confidence in your own ability to identify a healthy rabbit. You can tell when your kids are sick, right? You can also see whether a rabbit is sick or healthy. First, a healthy rabbit looks alert and responds to the movement and noise of your presence. A listless, droopy rabbit is probably seriously ill. Pick up the rabbit and check his face. The eyes should be clear and bright. There should be no matted or wet hair near the eyes which would indicate a discharge. Likewise there should be no matted or wet hair around or discharge from the nose. Check the teeth for proper alignment. You may need the breeder's help to hold the mouth open, but this is a reasonable request to make. The front teeth should be straight, with the top teeth overlapping the bottom ones. If any of the front teeth (which grow continuously) are angled off to one side, they will not wear down properly and eventually the animal will not be able to eat, or even close its mouth. Turn the rabbit over so that you can see its rear end. The breeder may have to help you with this as well if you are new at handling rabbits. Check that there is no fecal matter matted on its read end—a sign of diarrhea. Set the rabbit down on a table or in your lap and run your fingers over the entire body looking for lumps or tumors.

As a spinner, you want to check the quality of the fleece as well as the health of the rabbit. The rabbit you buy should not be matted. There may be small matts at the back of the neck behind the ears, and over the tail. A few tangles over the body are acceptable, but it is not wise to buy a rabbit which is heavily matted all over. Even if you can "clean it up", it will take hours of frustrating labor. It may indicate that the breeder doesn't take good care of his animals, or that this rabbit is one which has a genetic tendency to matt. Good animals often get badly matted because many people won't buy an angora unless it is in full coat. Therefore, the breeder postpones harvesting the fleece of a sale animal as long as possible. The result, of course, is matts.

Check the density of the fleece by blowing into it. Density is more important than length. You can hardly see the pink skin underneath a good, dense fleece. The fibers should be rather more silky than cottony, and if they have a little wavy crimp to them, that's great.

Registration and Pedigree

A breeder may advertise registered rabbits, supply pedigrees, or offer you "pet" quality rabbits. Though these categories vary greatly in price, none will guarantee you a good fiber-producing angora. So you should understand the differences. Most quality rabbits are sold by pedigree only. The pedigree is simply a piece of paper which records the ancestry of an individual rabbit. This form may be an "official" form from the ARBC or the NARBC, the breeder's own printed form, or even just a plain piece of paper. The pedigree should include the tattoo number of the rabbit, and the parents, grandparents, and great-grandparents, along with their tattoo numbers. (A tattoo number is a unique identifying number located in the rabbit's left ear.) The pedigree may also include information about the color of the ancestors, and perhaps their fiber production records, any awards they have won, and adult weight. (The latter is often omitted for angora rabbits, having more importance with the meat and show breeds.) Pedigrees should also be verified and signed by the breeder.

The registry system for rabbits in the United States is regulated by the ARBA and is substantially different from the more familiar systems used for dogs, cats, cattle, and so forth. Rabbits cannot be registered on the basis of parentage alone. In order to become registered, an official registrar from the ARBA must inspect the rabbit to see that it conforms to official standards. This takes extra effort, time, and money, and is usually done only for winning show animals. Registered animals usually cost more than others and registry does not guarantee good fiber production, because fiber production does not figure heavily in the various aspects of show competition. In addition, in order to win top show honors, a rabbit must win first prize in its breed at four separate shows. Angora rabbits do not win except when they are in full coat. Any rabbit which retains its full coat for the four- to six-month show season is not producing lots of fiber. The best show angora is a rabbit which produces a beautiful coat of fur and holds onto it for the show season, rather than shedding it off and growing a new one.

Another wrinkle in the registry business is that registrars are permitted to register rabbits in their own herd. Owners of large rabbitries often become registrars and register their own stock in order to save money on registration fees. Although economical for the breeder and doubtlessly used judiciously by most, the potential for abuse is obvious, especially when most spinners do not understand the system. This is not to say that you should not buy a registered rabbit, or that registered rabbits are not good animals or good fiber producers. Just be aware of what registration means.

"Pet quality" angoras may be a good choice for a handspinner. These are often excellent animals who have a minor show or breeding disqualification which may have nothing to do with fiber quality or production. Dropped ears or improperly colored toenails, for example, have absolutely no effect on the health of the rabbit or its fur. Crossbred angoras may also be considered as pet quality. "Crossbred" has an undeservedly negative connotation. First generation crossbreds between two purebred parents have a quality geneticists call hybrid vigor, and often are better animals than either parent. Of course, you would not want an angora crossed with a short-haired rabbit, but a cross between two angora breeds would be great. Pet-quality angoras may be sold without a pedigree or tattoo.

Buying From a Distant Source

If you do not live within driving distance of a breeder, you will have to have your new rabbit shipped to you. This can be expensive and seems more than a little risky, but my experiences with shipping rabbits by air have all been positive. In ten years of shipping rabbits all across the United States, I have had just two minor problems. On a short flight south, one bunny developed heat exhaustion. His new owner put a plastic gallon jug filled with cold water in his cage as an air conditioner, and by the next day he was fine. On another trip the rabbits missed their connecting flight. They arrived safely on a later flight, but their new owner had some anxious hours because the local airline officials didn't know where the rabbits were.

To the uninitiated, air-shipping rabbits can seem overwhelmingly complicated. However, the breeder/shipper from whom you are buying the rabbits is experienced and will do most of the work. Should you decide to buy your rabbit this way, the following information will let you know what to expect and how it is all arranged.

Airlines carefully regulate the conditions under which animals travel. Live animals fly "air freight" in environmentally controlled and pressurized baggage compartments. No animals are allowed to fly on days of extremely hot temperatures. I recall one summer when we waited well over a week for temperatures to drop below 90°F at Chicago O'Hare (no pun intended) so some bunnies could travel safely. Another summer, I had to wait until the end of September for Texas to cool down sufficiently to ship rabbits. The number of live animals traveling on any one flight is also limited so that they can be properly cared for. For example, I cannot ship rabbits on Tuesday, because my favorite airline handles regular Tuesday shipments of laboratory animals.

The cost of shipping live rabbits varies greatly with airline and distance traveled and connections made. Current charges to ship one to three rabbits range from a minimum of about $45 for a short flight to $120 for a cross-country journey. The airline insures the safety of the rabbits traveling on it. This extra risk and the special care live animals require contributes to the higher freight charges. The rabbit may be shipped prepaid, in which case you pay the breeder in advance for the shipping. If the rabbits are shipped collect, you pay the airlines when you pick up the rabbit.

Animals must travel in an airline-approved carrier. Requirements vary from airline to airline and it is often easier to buy an "air kennel" directly from the airline. A small kennel, suitable for one rabbit, costs about $35. It is sometimes cheaper to buy a carrying cage from a rabbit equipment supply company and have it shipped directly to the breeder, but you must be certain that it will arrive well in advance of the scheduled departure date and that it meets airline requirements.

Although veterinary certificates of health for traveling rabbits are not required by any government agency, most airlines require them anyway. This can add as much as $20 to the cost of each rabbit, even if the breeder doesn't charge you anything over the vet fee. However, it does insure that you will be receiving a healthy rabbit.

While the breeder takes care of most of the details, there are some things you should do. You will need to supply the breeder with your full name, address, and telephone number, as this information is required by the airline. You should also inform the breeder to which airport you want the rabbits delivered. Unless you live close to a major airport, you will want to give the breeder a couple of alternatives, if possible. It may be much less expensive to drive an extra hour or two to a larger airport than to pay for a short connecting flight. The breeder will arrange with you a mutually convenient day for shipping your rabbit. You should write down the name of the airline, the flight number, and the arrival time. Your rabbit will be ready for you to pick up about one hour after the plane has landed.

The air freight terminal where you pick up your rabbit is *not* the same as the passenger terminal where you pick up Grandmother. Airport signs will direct you to the location of the air freight terminal, which is often located at some distance from the passenger terminal. Parking at the air freight office is usually convenient and free. Enter the appropriate office and tell the employees that you are there to pick up a live rabbit. It is not a bad idea to have all the flight information on hand, though they will probably have no trouble locating your rabbit. Angora rabbits usually attract lots of attention even from jaded airline officials.

Whether you pick up your rabbit from the airport or from a local breeder, take your rabbit home with a minimum of fuss and delay, and put him in his new cage with plenty of fresh hay and water. You may look him over and hold him briefly, but then set him down and let him get some rest and get used to his new home. This is definitely not the time to let the children get to know the newest member of the household. You will have many more wonderful companionable days to spend with your new angora rabbit.

HABITATS

Angora rabbits have been raised in caves, colonies, and elaborate indoor warrens, as well as the more common wire cages and wooden hutches. Most angora rabbit raisers have decided opinions as to which arrangement is "best". I'll supply you with the basics on rabbit care, review with you the most common and easily obtainable types of dwellings, and let you make your own decision.

Housing must supply protection from the weather and from predators. Angora rabbits should not be exposed to drafts, extremes in temperatures (particularly heat), snow and rain, and direct sun. The amount of protection required will vary with your climate. However, heat bothers angoras more than cold. Remember they wear fur coats seven times warmer than sheep wool. Even 80° heat is uncomfortable, while 30° below zero in an unheated barn doesn't faze them.

Although rabbits should not be exposed to drafts of air blowing directly on them, they must have fresh clean air to breathe. The air should not smell musty, moldy, or stale. If the air smells fresh to you, then it is good for the rabbit as well. Too much humidity in the air is not desirable, as it seems to cause the hair to matt more easily as the rabbit moves about.

Cage Types

The easiest and most readily available housing facility for a pet angora rabbit is a free-standing wire cage. This popular type of cage is strong and sturdy, and provides ample protection from predators. A wire cage must be placed in a house or outbuilding in order to shelter the rabbit from the elements.

A drop pan located beneath the wire floor of the cage collects droppings and slides out for easy cleaning. If you line the drop pan with newspapers, clean-up becomes the simple matter of rolling up the newspapers and tossing them in the garbage. You can use rubber gloves for this chore to keep your hands clean. Keep a pair near the cage. How frequently you need to change the papers will depend on the proximity of the cage to your own daily living areas. A cage in the family room will have to be cleaned daily, while every other day or even twice weekly may suffice for a cage in the basement or garage. You might want to line the papers with a layer of sawdust, cedar shavings, or kitty litter to absorb moisture and control odors. A bacteriostatic sheet of paper created for this purpose and available from some rabbit supply companies has not had any noticeable effect on odor in the rabbit cages I have kept in the house. Be sure to keep the drop pan cleaned out regularly. Even if the odor doesn't bother you, ammonia fumes irritate the rabbit's eyes and the delicate linings of his nose, causing weeping and respiratory problems.

Cages like this one are convenient for spinners owning a single rabbit. Designed and built by the Klubertanz family, it features all wire construction, a drop pan and urine guards.
Photo courtesy of Klubertanz Equipment Company, Inc., Edgerton, WI 53534.

If you live in the country and have a barn or other outbuilding, you may choose an all-wire cage suspended from the ceiling. You can use heavy-duty wire of the kind used for electric fences to hang the cage. Be sure you use enough cross wires to give the cage stability. It shouldn't swing easily when bumped or when the rabbit moves around. The door to the cage should open outward, either out and down or out and to one side. A door opening inward startles the rabbit, who may perceive it as an attack. If you already have a cage with an inward opening door, you can remount the door with new clips from a rabbit supply company. These cages have no drop pan. The droppings fall to the floor and can be shoveled out weekly and placed on the compost pile. Sawdust or shavings spread on the floor beneath the cage help to absorb moisture.

Wire-bottom cages, whether free standing or suspended, were designed to allow the droppings to fall through the cage floor while still giving the rabbit something to stand on. The wire floor should have a 1 × ½ inch mesh. Droppings will not fall through a smaller mesh floor, and larger mesh does not support the rabbit's feet. Wire floors promote cleanliness but are uncomfortable for rabbits because of their delicate skin. Constant pressure of the wire can cause sores on a rabbit's feet which, like other health problems, reduces fiber production. One solution to this problem is to place a smooth wooden board in the cage, just large enough for the rabbit to sit on. Most rabbits will not soil the board (though they will probably chew on it).

The long angora hairs which the rabbit ingests when it grooms itself pass through the digestive system and these hairs connect the spherical droppings like pearls on a string. Needless to say, some of these strings catch on the wire floor so that the underside of the cage floor becomes festooned with little round droppings dangling by angora hair. To clean this up, you will need a wire bristle brush (available at any hardware store) to scrape the bottom of the cage periodically. This is much easier on the suspended cages than on the freestanding ones, which often have little clearance room beneath.

Old fashioned rabbit hutches were placed outdoors and made of solid wood with a door and a woven wire window. I had two banks of this sort on my farm and they worked well for angoras. So long as the rabbits were bedded on clean wheat straw and regularly groomed, their coats stayed nice and clean. The solid wood hutches protected the rabbits from the bitter north winds as well as the blazing summer sun. The woven wire window provided the perfect place for sunning on beautiful spring and autumn days. My hutches were oversized, which gave the rabbits plenty of room to move around, but also made it the devil to fetch one from the far back corner.

Outdoor wooden hutches may be constructed from plywood, but not from composition board or aspenite, which soften with exposure to the elements and rabbit urine. Eventually the rabbit will be able to gnaw escape holes. Designs for outdoor hutches can be found in general books on rabbit raising.

Clean straw should be placed in solid-bottom hutches to a depth of 4 to 6 inches. The rabbit will eat some of it, but this is okay because the straw is good roughage. The bedding should be cleaned out once a week and replaced with fresh straw. The old bedding can be bagged up and tossed out with the garbage, but the garden, if you have one, is a much better place for it. Rabbit manure is an excellent fertilizer and will not burn plants. One successful gardening book actually recommends keeping rabbits solely for the manure, which contains a good balance of nitrogen, potassium and phosphorus—the three major nutrients needed by plants. Most other animal manure contains only nitrogen.

Space, light, and safety

If you're a spinner with a single angora pet, you may keep your rabbit right in the house, which solves many of the weather-related problems. It may not solve the predator problems if you have an aggressive cat or a dog. Most pet dogs and cats get along well with a pet rabbit, but care must be taken especially when the rabbit is new to the household. To keep out predators, the rabbit cage must be made of solid wood or woven wire. Chicken wire will not suffice, as it can easily be torn open by dogs. Even hardware cloth cannot stop an aggressive dog if there is the least opening—such as a hole cut for a feeder or waterer. Better to be certain about the strength of your structure than be mourning your pet.

Use a light level in your rabbit's habitat that you find comfortable. Nonbreeding rabbits do not need a lot of light and probably don't like really bright lighting which makes them feel exposed and vulnerable. Rabbits have been raised in caves with virtually no light at all. Of course, you will need enough light to inspect and care for them.

To stay healthy, rabbits need some space to move around. The minimum amount of floor space necessary for a single adult angora is 4 square feet. Typical cage sizes range from the minimum to 30 × 36 inches, with 24 × 30 inches or 30 by 30 inches being most common. Eighteen inches in height is standard in this country. European breeders seem to prefer a taller cage—about 2 feet high. The rabbits do seem to appreciate the extra head room. They like to stretch up on their hind legs and look around.

A special consideration for angora rabbits is the protection of their fleece. The quickest way to ruin a fleece is to keep more than one rabbit in a single cage. Even with plenty of room to move about, the rabbits will damage each other's fleeces by rubbing against each other and matting the fibers. Sometimes a rabbit will even chew the fur off another rabbit.

You may hear discussions of the merits of raising rabbits in colonies. Some people think that it is more efficient to keep many angora rabbits in a single large pen or colony. However, this efficient only in terms of space. The goal of raising angora rabbits is *not* how many rabbits you can keep in a given space, but rather how much fiber—especially good quality fiber—you can produce. Colony raising was popular in the early stages of rabbit domestication, but it has long since been shown that the greatest production and highest quality fiber comes from rabbits which are housed individually.

For the innovative and adventurous, the possibilities for rabbit housing are unlimited. If your situation or frame of mind demands an alternative, by all means develop it. Any type of housing which meets the rabbit's basic needs will be satisfactory.

TRAVELLING WITH YOUR RABBIT

If you plan to take your rabbit with you when you travel, whether on vacation or to spinning meetings, you should probably invest in a carrying cage. A cardboard box lined with straw and with air holes will work, but if you travel very often you will find it inconvenient. A carrying cage should be just large enough for the rabbit to turn around in, but small enough to be easily carried.

Place the carrying cage in the car where it will not bounce around too much. It should not be in direct sun nor in the way of drafts from open windows or air conditioners. *Never* leave a rabbit or any pet inside a locked car. In even moderate temperatures a car in the sun—even with the windows cracked a few inches— quickly heats up to temperatures that kill.

Bring along a couple of empty shallow tin cans for food and water (for an extended trip). These can be wired to the sides of the cage to keep the rabbit from dumping them. Food and water are not necessary during actual travel time. The water will just spill and rabbits, like people, do not need to eat continuously. You may give the rabbit some hay or a slice of apple to nibble on while traveling.

FEEDING YOUR RABBIT

Feeding an adult angora presents something of a dilemma. Rabbits do not "self-regulate" their eating, and so only growing bunnies and lactating does can eat all they want and remain healthy. An adult rabbit needs to have its feed limited or it becomes fat and unhealthy. However, the adult angora rabbit is actively growing hair, which is largely protein. So you must provide a balance of good nutrition in the proper amounts for best fiber production.

I feed a pelletized rabbit food which is 18% protein. This feed is especially designed to meet the complete nutritional needs of rabbits, and I recommend it highly. I have used several brands and have not noticed any significant difference. The important factor is the percentage of protein. Common rabbit food has a protein content of 12%. This is too low to support a luxuriant growth of hair. Rabbit food with protein content of 20%, in my experience, has been too rich for some angoras, causing diarrhea. Eighteen percent seems just about right, and 16 to 17% protein is okay. Try to locate a farm supply feed store as a source for your pelletized rabbit food. Their prices are significantly lower than those of a pet store.

Rabbit food may be put in heavy crocks, but I prefer metal screen-bottomed feeders. These fit outside the cage, leaving more room inside the cage for the rabbit. They keep the feed clean, and the powdery residue present in all pelletized feed sifts out the bottom screen. These are available from rabbit equipment companies.

Like most domesticated animals, rabbits prefer a steady routine and like to be fed at the same time every day. Ideally, you should divide the rabbit's daily food ration by two and feed half in the morning and half in the evening. The rabbit quickly becomes habituated to your routine and when you make your appointed rounds and rattle the feed can, the rabbit will be watching you eagerly and waiting expectantly at the feeder.

Unless you are home nearly all the time, or live on a farm where other animals require it, you may find twice-daily care too demanding. Rest assured that your rabbit will do just fine being fed the entire amount once a day—preferably in the evening, since rabbits are more active at night. While rabbits prefer a routine, mine have adjusted to the erratic schedule of an entrepreneur. I feed them once a day, usually around the evening meal.

Adult angora rabbits (any breed) should be fed about 4 ounces of pellets per day, on average. This measures out to 2/3 cup. For maximum fiber production without endangering health, you can fine-tune feeding to your rabbit's hair growth cycle. For the first month after harvesting, give one or two extra tablespoons of feed. Give the normal amount for the second month. During the third month, when the rabbit has plenty of insulation and fiber growth has slowed, give one or two tablespoons less feed.

It is not a good idea to overfeed your rabbits. I like to keep my German angora rabbits to between 8 and 8½ pounds. Research has indicated that this is the ideal weight for the most efficient production of fiber. English angoras should weigh less than 6 pounds, French about 7 pounds. Overweight animals are more prone to diseases. European research even recommends not feeding angora rabbits at all for one day each week for improved appetite and health.

In addition to pelletized feed, angora rabbits should be fed clean, fresh-smelling grass hay. If the hay is moldy or dusty, do not use it for feed or bedding because it may cause respiratory problems for the rabbit. Regular feeding of hay is important mostly to add fiber to the diet. The pellets, which are composed primarily of alfalfa, have been steamed and treated so that much of the roughage has been broken down.

Hay is also a real treat for the rabbit. Rabbits love to nibble on the sweet-smelling grasses. It is fun to watch the long grass stem disappear into the rabbit's mouth, much in the same way a person sucks in strands of spaghetti. I even watched two bunnies eating a single stem, their mouths getting closer and closer, just like in a cartoon. Hay can be fed as often as once a day, or as little as once a week. It can be purchased at the same feed store where you buy your rabbit food.

Feeding "treats" seems to be one of the most rewarding aspects of having a pet, but it is one which usually is not good for the animal. Try to limit yourself to giving only healthy treats. My angora rabbits really appreciate a half a slice of *dry* white bread every now and then. The bread must be dry in order for them to be able to chew off pieces. They like whole wheat bread too, but don't like rye. If fed pellets, hay, and dry bread all the same time, they will eat the bread first.

Rabbits also are enthusiastic about the chewable papaya tablets that some angora raisers believe prevent wool block. An occasional tablet doesn't seem to harm the rabbits and they certainly like them.

Other healthy treats for your rabbit include whole grains such as oats, wheat, or barley. It is best to give only a teaspoon or two per day because these grains are relatively low in protein. Cracked corn is high in energy and I don't recommend feeding it except to rabbits housed outdoors in extremely cold weather (below zero).

Calf Manna is a high-protein supplement which is sometimes recommended for lactating does. However, this supplement is too rich for an adult rabbit on commercial pellets and should not be given for fear of causing intestinal disorders.

You may feed limited amounts of fresh greens with caution. Rabbits have a ruminant system something like that of cows or sheep. Much of the actual digestion of food is done by intestinal bacteria, and their internal balance and functioning can be dramatically disrupted by the abrupt introduction of large amounts of fresh food. This results in diarrhea, bloat, and possibly death. Another problem with fresh greens is that they spoil rapidly. Large piles of greens may ferment and the toxins in the deteriorating vegetation may harm the rabbit. Some angora breeders successfully feed many different greens to their rabbits. If you're a novice, however, you should be aware of the risks.

Rabbits do not require fresh food in their diet. If you want to give some as a treat, an inch or two of carrot, or a quarter of a small apple will do. Other fresh foods which may be given safely are branches from apple trees, celery leaves, mangels, and comfrey—although the fuzzy comfrey leaves tend to get caught in the fleece. Remove wilted greens from the cage promptly.

A single rabbit kept for your own fiber production probably does not require vitamin supplements, but if you want to provide them, water soluble vitamins for rabbits are available. Depending on the rest of their diet, rabbits may or may not need extra salt. It's good insurance to put little spools of salt in the rabbit's cage. Some rabbits will gnaw on them and some won't.

Be alert for signs that your rabbit has stopped eating. When you give your rabbit his feed, pellets from the previous feeding should be gone, or nearly so. If most of the feed is left, this may be a sign of illness. Empty the feeder of remaining food. A rabbit which doesn't feel much like eating is certainly not interested in stale food. Put half the usual ration of fresh pellets in the feeder and give plenty of fresh sweet hay and water, and perhaps a slice of dry white bread. So long as the rabbit is drinking water and nibbling at hay or bread, probably everything is, or will be, okay. A rabbit's appetite varies, just as yours does. The next day, the half-ration of pellets will probably be gone and you can resume regular feeding. What to do if the rabbit doesn't eat at all is discussed later in this chapter. This points out another advantage of feeding measured amounts of food. If your rabbit has a full feeder in front of him at all times, he may become seriously ill before you notice that he is not eating.

There are many alternatives to feeding rabbits commercial pellets. One of the more reasonable of these alternatives is to feed high-protein alfalfa hay in conjunction with whole grains and mineral supplements. One German book recommends a mash of potato skins, legumes, fruit peelings, wheat flour and dried herbs, among other less palatable ingredients. Some diets even include large amounts of fresh material such as comfrey and root vegetables. Many rabbit breeders in this country seem to take pride in developing new rabbit formulas.

Rabbit raising professionals around the world agree that commercial rabbit feeds are superior to homemade combinations in terms of convenience and fiber production. In areas of the world where alternative feeds are still commonly used, the main reason cited is the expense and lack of availability of the pelletized feed. Even in these areas, special rabbits, such as breeding does and growing bunnies, are fed pellets if the owner can afford them. In the U.S., rabbit pellets are not outlandishly expensive. There is no reason for a spinner to go to a lot of extra trouble when there exists a readily available, complete rabbit ration which is convenient, nutritious, and affordable. You can provide variety in your rabbit's diet by feeding small amounts of healthy treats as discussed earlier.

Even more important than food is clean, fresh water, which should be available to the rabbit at all times. A rabbit will die more quickly from lack of potable water than from lack of food. This is especially true for domestic rabbits fed on commercial pellets. These dry pellets require increased amounts of water for digestion.

The value of water is often underestimated and is especially difficult for children to understand. I have heard of cases in which children were entrusted with the care of the rabbits. After the rabbits died, the parents discovered that although the child fed the rabbits daily, the water was never replenished.

Water for your rabbit should be clean enough that you would drink it yourself. It should be cool, except in winter, when rabbits housed outdoors should be given warm water. Change the water daily. It is not okay just to top off a bowl of stale, dirty water. In the winter, rabbits kept outdoors where water freezes should be given fresh, warm water at least three times each day.

A rabbit will drink out of a water bottle or a crock. For the spinner with an individual rabbit, I recommend a water bottle such as those used for guinea pigs or gerbils and available at any pet store. You do have to unscrew the cap and replace the water daily, but the water stays clean. If you choose a crock you must clean it daily. The crock must be heavy and flat bottomed. A bowl will not suffice because the rabbit will quickly dump it over. An open crock of water easily becomes contaminated with feed, droppings, and hay as the rabbit moves about his cage. There are automatic watering systems available which are convenient and insure your rabbit a fresh supply of water directly from your own plumbing, but they are generally too elaborate and expensive for just one rabbit.

With a large water bottle or automatic watering system you are able to go away overnight or for a weekend and leave your rabbit unattended. If you were to be gone, say, from Friday night to Sunday night, you would make sure there was one large bottle or several smaller ones (enough for a quart of water), and two days' ration of feed in the feeder along with plenty of fresh hay in the cage. When you come back on Sunday night, you would feed the rabbit as usual and change the water. This is not an ideal system, and I am not advocating routine neglect of your rabbit, but in a crunch this will work with no adverse effects on the rabbit.

RABBIT DISEASE

Before I began my adventure in farming, I brought a book on veterinary medicine and animal care and read it cover to cover. After reading that book, I developed the worst case of cold feet about getting into the farming business. There were millions of things that could go wrong with live animals! Gradually I came to realize that in spite of the many diseases and afflictions of all animals—humans included—most survive and thrive.

It is much easier to prevent an illness than to cure one. I can't overemphasize the importance of a sanitary environment, clean food and water, and fresh air (without drafts). Keep a sharp eye on your rabbit, so you notice any peculiarities right away. You will have far fewer problems with single rabbit than a breeder will with dozens or hundreds of animals. The more rabbits you have in one place, the greater the chances for infection and contagion. If your rabbit does become ill, the sooner you recognize and treat the problem, the better your chances for success. You can easily solve many health problems yourself. A few illnesses are usually fatal even with the intervention of a good veterinarian.

If your angora rabbit does become sick, first contact the breeder from whom you bought the animal—not to complain, but to request advice. Rabbit breeders are more likely to be familiar with common rabbit diseases and can tell you how to treat them. Unfortunately, there has been relatively little research on rabbit disease in this country. In commercial herds it is usually more economical to dispose of a sick rabbit than to treat it. As a result, most veterinarians have little experience with rabbits, though a good vet's advice may be helpful.

Rabbits are generally free of most of the debilitating and fatal diseases of other pets, including rabies and distemper. The most devastating rabbit disease, *myxomatosis,* is almost unheard of in this country, although it is common in Europe. In the United States, the most dread rabbit diseases are the contagious bacterial respiratory infections, commonly called *snuffles.* A rabbit with snuffles sneezes often and has a runny discharge from its nose. Even when treated it recurs again and again in the same rabbit. Most serious rabbit raisers don't even treat snuffles— they eliminate the rabbit immediately. If your rabbit doesn't have snuffles when you buy it and you have no other rabbits, chances are that you will never have to deal with this problem.

Wool block is a common and serious problem for angora rabbits. Wool block is an intestinal blockage formed by a plug of hair, mucus, and food—similar to a hair ball in cats. It blocks the digestive system and if not treated promptly, the rabbit will die. However, *it is preventable.*

Commonly believed to result from a rabbit's ingestion of hair during self-grooming, recent research at the French National Angora Laboratory has demonstrated that wool block is caused primarily by overfeeding. Angoras fed unrestricted diets of pellets developed wool block regularly, whereas rabbits on limited feed did not. In the hundreds of rabbits I have raised, I have had only two cases of wool block and both rabbits were on increased feed. You can avoid wool block by controlling your rabbit's food supply.

The first, most obvious sign of wool block is that the animal stops eating completely and also stops defecating. Activity decreases. A rabbit with wool block will often sit huddled in the back of the cage. On examination, you will find no signs of diarrhea. If you palpate the abdomen gently, you will be able to feel a large mass. Begin treatment immediately. The success rate of treatment is higher the sooner it is started. Mineral oil, administered orally with an eye dropper, 1 teaspoon per day, is the traditional treatment for wool block. Mineral oil is just a lubricant. Greater success can be achieved by using naturally occurring enzymes which will break down the mass. Health food stores now carry papaya and pineapple enzyme tablets which break down protein and vegetable matter. Give five or six of these tablets per day until the problem is corrected. If you cannot find any enzyme tablets, fresh or frozen pineapple juice will supply one of the enzymes. (Canned pineapple juice will not work because heating destroys the enzymes.) During treatment you can also gently palpate and massage the mass to help mechanically to break it down. You will know when the blockage is disintegrated because the rabbit will perk up, and begin eating and defecating again.

Ear mites are another common ailment you can easily treat at home. These microscopically small parasites burrow under the skin in the rabbit's ears, causing itching and irritation. Symptoms include scratches and scaly scabs in the ears. If left untreated, these become infected and infections can spread to the inner ear, where they become exceedingly difficult to treat successfully.

If caught early, treatment consists merely of putting a few drops of mineral oil into each ear. The oil covers the air holes of the mites' burrows and so suffocates them. Hold the ear closed and massage the base of the ear gently to spread the oil around. Repeat the treatment every day for ten days and then again two weeks later to catch the next hatching of mite eggs. If the situation does not respond to mineral oil, or the infestation is severe, ask your veterinarian for a medicine used for dogs or cats with ear mites. This medication has an insecticide to kill the mites plus an antibiotic to treat secondary infections, and it works well on rabbits. Put the medication in the ears according to label directions. Occasionally mites are also found between the ears and on the back just behind the ears. Here it is a good idea to clip the hair off the infected area before applying the medication.

Scours (diarrhea) rarely occurs in adult rabbits. The most common causes are over-feeding, feeding food too rich, or feeding too many greens, thereby disrupting the delicate balance of intestinal flora. An animal with diarrhea becomes dehydrated and the electrolyte balance in the body is disrupted. These conditions can rapidly become fatal.

Soft droppings with a bad smell are an early sign of diarrhea. Eventually, the fecal matter becomes a formless mass and the hind end of the animal will be matted with smelly feces. "Night droppings" produced by healthy rabbits in the very early morning are sometimes mistaken for diarrhea because they are soft with a sticky mucus coating. Night droppings are not true waste products and are usually ingested by the rabbit before you see them.

The best you can do to treat diarrhea is to remove *all* pelletized feed and greens. Give the rabbit only grass hay and water. This is the equivalent of the dry toast and tea that your mother gave you when had a tummy ache. If the diarrhea is severe, you may try giving the rabbit some Kaopectate, which helps prevent water loss, and putting electrolyte replacement powder in the water to restore the electrolyte balance. If the rabbit does not improve within 24 to 48 hours, or if the situation worsens, there is probably nothing that can be done.

Conjunctivitis, or weepy eye, is an infection which causes a liquid discharge or weepy appearance to the eye. I never saw it until I got German angoras. The first line of German angoras I imported from Canada seemed to have a genetic disposition for this problem. A veterinarian can supply you with an ophthalmic ointment. To apply this ointment you must hold the rabbit tightly. Lift the upper eyelid and squeeze a line of ointment about 1/3 of an inch long and let it drop onto the eye. As you let the rabbit close his eye, try to gently nudge the ointment under the lid. That's all there is to it. The blinking of the eye will distribute the medication effectively.

Rabbits raised on wire bottom cages sometimes develop sore on their feet which rabbit raisers call sore hock. Get the rabbit off the wire immediately and provide him with a solid-floor cage with clean straw bedding. Treat any open wounds with a disinfectant such as hydrogen peroxide and then cover with an over-the-counter antibiotic ointment. Inspect the wound and treat daily. Take special care to see that the bedding is clean and dry. If caught in time, the sores will eventually heal. However, I would not put this rabbit back into a cage with a wire floor.

Rabbits do not often get intestinal worms, but if you have dogs or cats, worms can become a problem. If you suspect worms or other intestinal parasites because of listlessness or unthriftiness, take a fecal sample to your veterinarian for examination.

Rabbits have a variety of other possible disorders. Most of these are associated with pregnancy and birth or affect only very young rabbits, so you will not have to worry about any of these problems with your pet angora. Unless you are raising many angoras as a business, I recommend you refrain from breeding them. Breeding introduces complications of pregnancy and delivery, diseases of young bunnies, extra time, effort, and expense. Breeding decreases fiber production because pregnant or lactating does cannot waste energy and resources on hair growth.

Too much emphasis in this country is placed on producing more angora rabbits, and not nearly enough on producing more fiber. In France, 80% of angora does are *never* bred. It is considered a sacrifice to have to breed the does enough to ensure herd replacement. We would do well to follow this example.

GROOMING AND FIBER HARVESTING

Some people are blessed with a special gift for working with animals. Animals seem instinctively to trust them. I know one such woman. She can pick up her rabbits any which way—under the front legs, as you would pick up a young child under the arms, for instance. She can carry two large German angoras in her arms at once with no trouble, because they offer no resistance. The rabbits lie languidly upside down in her lap as she grooms their bellies and clips fur from their feet. I've never seen her rabbits frantic, never seen them lash out with their powerful hind feet or try to wriggle away from her.

I don't have that sort of talent, I'm sorry to say, and unless you do, you will need to learn a few things about handling your rabbit. Rabbits are timid creatures, so do everything you can to provide them with a feeling of safety and security. Always be gentle and kind. Speak to your rabbit in a low, soothing voice. Avoid loud noises and sudden movements which startle rabbits and make them nervous. Being lifted into the air is scary, so when you pick up a rabbit, give it the security of good support. Likewise, being turned onto its back puts the rabbit into a vulnerable position which it doesn't like. Your handling should be as consistent as possible. This way the rabbit knows what to expect. Adding a healthy treat to the end of a handling session may also be helpful. Whenever you're handling your rabbit, whether it be to carry him somewhere, groom him, or pluck his fur, be prepared to stop and put him back in his cage if he becomes frightened, restless, or uncomfortable. Don't turn handling into a power struggle. That is a situation in which you both lose.

It is a good idea to wear long sleeves to keep from getting scratched when handling your rabbit, because his feet may flail about when you pick him up. New rabbit owners are often greatly surprised at the strength of those hind feet and the sharpness of the toenails. You may also want to wear a lightweight nylon jacket (I use an old windbreaker) to keep your clothes clean. Angora fiber doesn't stick to the nylon.

The proper way to hold a rabbit is illustrated here. Rabbits are a little like ostriches in that they feel safer if they can hide their heads. In this position, the rabbit's feet are supported by your right arm and hip, and his head is tucked under your right elbow. Place your left hand on the rabbit's back for security.

If your rabbit is really quite comfortable with you, you can hold him vertically. Here, the rabbit's hind legs and bottom are supported on your right arm and hip while his front legs rest on your right shoulder. In this friendly position, the rabbit can look around, nuzzle your ear, and generally be companionable.

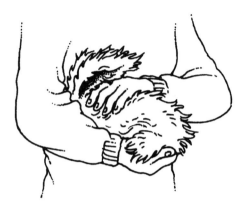

The proper way to carry an angora rabbit. The rabbit feels safer with its head tucked under your arm. One hand resting on the back provides safety and security.

An alternate way to hold a calm, friendly rabbit.

To get a rabbit into either of these positions, pick him up by the nape of the neck, smoothing the ears down along the back under your hands. Immediately place the other hand underneath him for support. Then you can tuck his head under your arm or let him stretch up onto your shoulder. Don't ever pick up a rabbit by the ears or by his fur.

Your rabbit will be friendlier and easier to handle if you groom him often. I recommend that you reserve 20 minutes or half an hour at a regular time each week for grooming, combing, and plucking. If you make it a regularly scheduled time you are more likely to do it. I emphasize this point because the greatest source of failure in raising angoras is putting off the combing and plucking until it is too late and you have a rabbit that is full of matts. This is frustrating for you and painful for the rabbit, and you don't get any fiber out of it. A bad deal all the way around.

Grooming the rabbit at least once a week will keep the fleece and furnishings long and silky-smooth. You will also be able to keep your rabbit used to being handled and catch any early signs of disease, so pick a time when you will be able to devote yourself to your pet. Choose a spot that is comfortable, and turn on some music or a favorite radio program, so that the time is an enjoyable highlight in your otherwise hectic week.

Angoras do not really *require* weekly grooming, and in a commercial rabbitry they are not so well cared for. But here is another advantage you have over a commercial enterprise. You can give your rabbit the extra loving care that really makes a difference. You can keep him in superb condition so that you not only get the most in terms of fiber production, but in personal satisfaction as well.

Grooming

You will probably be comfortable grooming your rabbit in your lap. Use an old towel or piece of carpeting to protect your clothes and give the rabbit secure footing. A metal dog comb with medium teeth works well for general grooming. A fine-toothed comb is handy for furnishings. Some combs have medium teeth on one end and fine teeth on the other. I like to start combing on the front of the rabbit's left side, but you can start anywhere that is comfortable for you and the rabbit. Combing over the top of the fleece will not suffice because angora fur is too dense. I've seen angora rabbits beautifully brushed in appearance, but covered with matts underneath. You must comb the fur in layers, beginning with the undermost layers. Hold the uncombed fur up away from the rabbit's body while you comb each layer of fur out and down. This motion reminds me of the layered "teasing" that many girls did with their hair when I was in high school, except with the opposite effect. You want to comb out the tangles, not put them in. When you get one section combed through from the belly to the backbone, start another section and work your way around the rabbit in this manner. The point here is to comb out the loose fibers and remove any matts, but not pull out still-growing, well-rooted fibers.

Combing out the belly fur is a little tricky. If your rabbit doesn't protest, turn him onto his back and cradle him between your legs. In this position, you can comb out the belly and even tend to the fur on the legs. Unfortunately, most rabbits do not like this position, which makes them feel vulnerable and scared. If you can't coax your rabbit into lying on his back, you can reach the belly fur, albeit not as easily, with the rabbit still on his feet. With the rabbit facing your right, align your left forearm so that it is parallel to his body and near his belly. Holding the rabbit close to your body, use gentle, firm pressure to sort of scoop the rabbit up just enough so that you can comb through half of the belly fur with the comb in your right hand. To do the other side, reverse the process. To groom the fur under the chin and chest, hold the rabbit in the same position, only this time, lift his head gently while you comb out the fur beneath it. Use extra care when combing out the furnishings on the ears, which are quite fragile and could tear if you comb too hard. I have heard that you can actually put the comb right through the tender skin at the tip of the ears if you are not careful. Although it will have to be carded or blended, you will want to save the fiber that comes off when you comb the rabbit.

The regular weekly grooming session is also a good time to check the toenails, which must be clipped every few months. A regular dog nail clipper, available at any pet store, works well for this task. You want to cut off only the dead part of the nail. The quick, or living, part of the nail is pink and will bleed if you cut into it. The pink quick is readily apparent on white rabbits, but you will have to look hard on some colored rabbits, where the pink color is hidden under colored toenails.

Harvesting Fiber

About four times a year (every 13 weeks) the angora fiber on your rabbit is ready to be harvested. At this time, most of the hair follicles have ceased actively growing and the root of the hair loosens so that it is easily removed. Stray fibers collecting in the corners of the cage and clumps of hair falling away in strings from the rabbit's fleece are indications that the fiber is ready to be harvested.

There are three basic methods of harvesting angora: plucking, shearing, and combing. Choose your method based on the fiber characteristics described earlier and the results that you want to see in your finished yarns and garments.

Plucking

Plucking yields the highest quality fiber for handspinning. Begin by assembling all the equipment you will need, including a metal dog comb and a pair of stainless steel surgical scissors or small sewing scissors. Other combs and scissors may work, but these are what I use. You also need some containers to put the various grades of angora into. I have found empty Quaker Oats boxes convenient for this purpose. It is easier to sort the fiber into grades as you pluck. Tape a ruler nearby until you can "eyeball" the proper length. A waste can nearby is helpful for any fiber, matted or stained, that you feel is not worth saving. Send the kids outside and unplug the phone. Put on your favorite music or radio show to keep your mind entertained while your hands are busy.

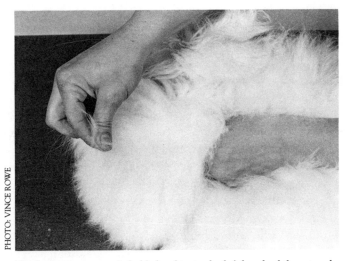

PHOTO: VINCE ROWE

To pluck angora wool, hold the skin in the left hand while using the thumb and forefinger of the right hand to gently pull out a small amount of wool.

If you want to pluck with the rabbit sitting in your lap, find a comfortable chair and place your equipment and containers on a nearby table within easy reach. I prefer to stand when plucking my rabbits. I use a table at a height that doesn't require stretching up or hunching over. A square of carpet remnant gives the rabbit a secure place to sit, and I keep the plucking equipment on a shelf nearby.

Some angora raisers like to tie their rabbit to a plucking board for harvesting fiber. A plucking (or shearing) board consists of a wooden board about 18 × 24 inches, with a nail or hook at each end. The rabbit is stretched out on the board and soft strips of material are used to tie his legs to either end. Some people tie just one leg to the board. Others tie all four legs, and some tie one front leg and the opposite back leg. The rabbits do relax and become habituated to it.

Modern commercial rabbitries in Europe have specially designed, pivoting plucking tables with adjustable heights. The rabbits are tied by one front foot and one hind foot so that they are stretched lengthwise on the table. Troughs on either side of the table are used to collect and sort the angora fiber. French angora raisers use a plucking knife to harvest angora, which makes the plucking very fast and painless for the fingers and thumb of the plucker. Leslie Samson in Canada uses a variation of the French method she calls "strip combing". She plucks angora by grabbing the fiber tips between thumb and comb. Large amounts of fiber can be harvested quickly with either method, but both cause the tips to become tangled, which interferes with controlled drafting. In order to get the very best fiber for handspinning, you will have to rely on your thumb and forefinger. If one or both of these become sore you can cushion them with a bandage or a finger cot from a medical supplier.

For best results, you should first comb the fleece thoroughly, removing all tiny matts and tangles. Follow the previous guidelines for grooming. A lot of good fiber will come out in your comb and you may be tempted not to "waste" it. However, this combed fiber will not spin as readily as the aligned plucked fibers, so save it separately. When the rabbit is completely combed, you are ready to pluck.

The hair comes out most easily from the sides of the rabbit, and so begin plucking there. With your left hand, grab a small section of skin. This provides support for the skin while, with the thumb and first finger of your right hand, you pluck out a small tuft of fibers. Pull in the same direction the fur lies on the rabbit, usually down and toward the rear. Once you are familiar with the plucking motion, you will find that you can make several pluckings in succession, harvesting quite a bit of angora, before you place it in its appropriate container. However, you should never take more than a little bit with each tug. Pluck one bit, then lift up your thumb very briefly, just long enough to grab another bit and tug again to pull out the second bit without dropping the first. You can repeat this procedure several times before there is too much fiber between your thumb and forefinger to get a sufficient grip on the next bit. The fibers should come out easily, without hurting the rabbit, although some rabbits do appear to be ticklish on some areas. Repeat this plucking procedure until you have covered the entire body. Stomach fibers are rarely plucked, although they are sometimes long enough on German angoras to make plucking them worthwhile. Furnishings are never plucked.

At first it may take you 45 minutes to pluck an angora, but with practice you should be able to pluck a French or English angora in good condition in 15 or 20 minutes, harvesting three or four ounces of angora. The German angoras may take an hour to an hour and a half. Repeated combing through each section of fur just before it is plucked seems to make it come out more easily. Some fibers may not come out, even with this encouragement. This is because the follicular growth cycles are not synchronous. You can try to get the rest off in a few days, or next week.

Because a second growth cycle usually starts before the long fibers are plucked, you will probably not pluck the rabbit bare, although it will look small and rather naked when you are finished.

Unless your rabbit is outdoors in cold weather, it doesn't hurt to pluck it bare. You should definitely remove all the fiber which is ready to come out. Once loosened at the root, the hair will come out anyway and will matt if you don't take it. I had one white doe who would pluck herself stark naked—like a pink-skinned baby. The only hair left on her entire body was a little bit behind her neck and a meager line down her back where she couldn't reach. The mounds of angora she removed from her body were far too much for her nest. It was summer and with all that extra insulation, the heat would have killed the babies, so I had to take most of it away. (And I couldn't use it because it was mixed up with the hay from the nest box.) The self-plucking behavior is due to the rabbit's maternal instincts and some does with strong instincts can go overboard.

Once you have plucked a rabbit down to bare skin, do not be alarmed if you do not immediately see a new growth of hair. Hair growth begins deep within the hair follicle, beneath the surface of the skin. It may be a week or two before you can see the new hairs coming in. A good angora rabbit will have a full coat ready for plucking in another 13 weeks.

Shearing

Shearing or clipping involves actually cutting the fiber rather than pulling it out by the roots. It can be done with electric pet clippers, scissors, or manual shears. Even if you routinely pluck your rabbit, there may be times that you will need or want to shear. I usually clip off the first fleece of baby angora which is too fine and "cottony" to be used as prime. Shearing also protects the tender skin of a young angora. You also might want to clip the fleece off your angora during a dangerous heat spell. Or you may be accumulating fiber for a blending project.

Whatever the reason, you will want to set yourself up much as you would for plucking comfortably with materials in easy reach. You will need a pair of sharp scissors for the clipping. For a long time I used a pair of 4-inch stainless steel surgical scissors. Now I have a pair of pet barbering scissors. The curlicue on the end keeps the back of my fingers from getting sore. I have seen other people use everything from sewing scissors to huge black kitchen shears. Available in Germany are scissors equipped with a guard which helps to prevent accidental cuts into the skin and leaves a short layer of fur on the rabbit for cold weather protection. Electric pet clippers with a special "angora head" are available too. They are something like electric sheep shears. However, they are fairly expensive and probably not worthwhile for just one rabbit. Once I found at a yard sale some old fashioned manual hair clippers such as were used for barbering men's hair. They worked quite well.

Second cuts and cutting the rabbit's tender skin are two of the pitfalls of shearing. As with sheep shearing, it is more useful to hold the skin down firmly as you clip, rather than pull up on the hair. If you pull up on the hair, you pull up the skin as well, making it much more likely that you will cut into it. Clip slowly and carefully until you learn the contours of the rabbit's body. Small nicks in the skin—which you probably will get—may make you sick with horror, but actually will heal quickly all by themselves. A larger cut should be treated with an antibiotic cream or spray.

Second cuts reduce fleece quality. Keep in mind when you are shearing that the end product is the longest, most uniform fleece possible, not an evenly clipped rabbit. If your clipping is uneven and you don't want your rabbit to look like it got a real hack job at the barber's, wait until after you have clipped off the good fleece and put it aside. Then you can trim the rabbit up as you desire.

I have often read that to begin shearing you should part the hair down the back of the rabbit. You might be able to do this on a French angora with little hair, but you sure can't part the hair on the back of one of my German angoras so that you can see the skin. To start shearing a densely fleeced rabbit you must dive right in with the scissors or shears at the back of the head and clip straight down the back. Don't pull off the loose fleece; just move down the side, clipping off layer after layer. The shorn fleece holds together lightly and curls out and away as you shear.

When you get to the belly, stop for a moment to put the already-shorn fleece in a container. Next shear across the rump and then turn the rabbit around and shear the other side. The neck, chest and belly can be reached in the same manner as for plucking. When you shear the belly, take care not to clip a doe's teats or, farther down between the hind legs, a buck's scrotum. Generally speaking, you want to clip the hair as close to the skin as possible. However, if your rabbit is kept outside during very cold weather, it is advisable to leave 1/4 to 1/2 inch of hair to keep the rabbit warm.

The furnishings do not grow as quickly as the body hair. If you like the furnishings, don't clip them off or you will have months and months of disappointment before they grow back. On the other hand, if you are the pragmatic type, you can clip those furnishings right down and you won't be bothered with them again for a good long time.

Combing

Combing the fleece is the oldest, most traditional method of harvesting angora. The combing process simply removes whatever fibers are loose at the time. This is the way that cashmere is harvested from goats in the Himalayas. The goats tend to shed their undercoat more or less all at the same time (in the spring), whereas early angora rabbits had irregular follicular cycles and only a little of the fiber could be harvested at one time. Rabbits had to be combed regularly and often. The process was tedious, but afforded the only reasonable way to harvest the valuable fiber.

Combed angora contains many tangled fibers which do not draft easily. Lightly carded combings (so long as there are no matts) spin into a respectable angora yarn and of course, combings work well in carded blends. Although this is not the most efficient way to harvest angora, I know of several angora raisers who find this more pleasant and less stressful than plucking.

A major concern of angora raisers is matted fleece. Matts should be avoided at all costs. Excessive matting can be caused by genetic factors, high humidity, or illness. If your rabbit matts up even with weekly grooming, it probably has a genetic tendency to matt and should not be kept. It is my opinion that the most common cause of excessive matts is the failure to groom the rabbit and pluck the fibers when they are ready. Once the hairs mature, the roots loosen. The loose hairs are held in the fleece by other, still-rooted hairs. The movement of the rabbit will tangle them until they are felted solid. When you allow your rabbit to become matted, you have wasted not only valuable fiber, but also your time. It takes much longer to clip off those dreadful matts just to throw them away than it does to pluck the rabbit at the proper time.

The matted fur collects moisture and dirt, which the rabbit can't clean away. The skin under the matts can become irritated and sores may develop after the rabbit scratches. If the sores become infected, then you have real problems. Avoid this situation with proper grooming and timely harvesting.

Storing Your Fiber

Keeping your angora fiber in good spinnable condition is just as important as harvesting it properly. However you choose to store your fiber, you will have better results if you try to keep the fibers aligned as much as possible, avoid compressing them, and protect them from moths. There is no point in spending all this time, money and effort producing the best-quality angora fiber, only to have it become matted beyond recognition or go to feed moth larvae.

Angora fiber should be stored loosely. I have seen enormous volumes of angora crammed into a tiny sandwich bag. It doesn't take long for the fibers under pressure to become beaten down and lifeless, or matted ever so slightly, but enough to make drafting difficult. I have also seen paper bags of angora literally teeming with wool moth larvae, which chew the long, lovely fibers to lint. Some people recommend storing angora in boxes or even paper bags with tissue paper between layers of angora. This seems to work well to preserve the loft, although I would further enclose the whole package in a plastic bag to protect it from moths or store it carefully in a cedar chest with moth balls.

I store my angora in gallon-sized self-sealing plastic bags, 3 ounces to a bag. I zip the bags shut with plenty of air to keep the fiber from compacting. This method allows the fiber to maintain its loft and gives protection from moths. I have heard that it is not advisable to store angora in plastic, but I have been doing it successfully for more than ten years. (Of course, the fiber must be dry.) Some of my angora has been stored in this manner for years with no adverse effects.

Keep your silky angora fibers safely stored until you are ready to create your own soft fluffy yarns and then into the angora project of your dreams. It all begins with the rabbit you raise yourself.

Happy Spinning!

Selected Bibliography

Fannin, Allen. *Handspinning: Art & Technique*. New York: Van Nostrand Reinhold, 1970.

Gayot, E. *Lièvres, Lapins et Léporides*. Paris: Librairie de la Maison Rustique, 1865.

Knutson, Linda. *Synthetic Dyes for Natural Fibers*. Loveland, Colorado: Interweave Press, 1986.

Lebas, F., P. Coudert, R. Rouvier, and H. de Rochambeau. *The Rabbit: Husbandry, Health and Production*. Rome: Food and Agriculture Organization of the United Nations, 1986.

Lynne, Erica. "Sandstorm". *Cast-On*, ix:26 (Spring, 1990), 12–14.

Lynne, Erica. *see also* Rowe, Erica.

Morey, Nancy. *Rainbow Dyeing: A Multicolor Approach to Dyeing*. Binghamton, New York: All Ready, Inc., 1987.

Raven, Lee. *Hands On Spinning*. Loveland, Colorado: Interweave Press, 1987.

Rowe, Erica. "Handspun Angora Mittens". *Spin·Off*, viii:1 (Spring, 1984), 51.

_____. "Rainbow Dyeing". *The Weaver's Journal*, viii:2 (Fall, 1983), 31–35.

_____. "Angoras". *Rabbits*, vi:5 (May, 1983), 12–13.

Vinroot, Sally, and Jennie Crowder. *The New Dyer*. Loveland, Colorado: Interweave Press, 1981.

Rabbits Breeders' Organizations and Publications

American Rabbit Breeders Association (ARBA): P.O. Box 426, Bloomington, Illinois 61702. This organization provides a book, A *Progressive Program for Raising Better Rabbits and Cavies*, to its members.

National Angora Rabbit Breeders Club (NARBC): This ARBA affiliate has no permanent address. Contact ARBA for current club secretary address.

"Domestic Rabbits". Bloomington, Illinois: ARBA.

Index